THE UNEXPECTED TRUTH

THE UNEXPECTED TRUTH

Live & Survive & Live Again
LASALA

By
Oluwafemi Senu

LASALA

OLUWAFEMI SENU

2022

Copyright © 2009-2022 by Oluwafemi Senu

All rights reserved. This book or any portion thereof may not be reproduced or used in any manner whatsoever without the express written permission of the publisher except for the use of brief quotations in a book review or scholarly journal.

First version: Published by Author House-Dec. 16, 2009
Second version: Published by Blub-Nov. 16, 2014
Third version: Published by Oluwafemi Senu -Dec.01, 2022

ISBN 978-1-907783-11-1

LASALA Foundation
Suite 43, 64 Willoughby Lane, N17 0SP
London, United Kingdom

Join me on Facebook: https://www.facebook.com/oluwafemisenubooks
Email the Author direct at: lasalafoundation@gmail.com
Twitter: @oluwafemi_senu

Ordering Information:
Special discounts are available on quantity purchases by corporations, associations, educators, and others. For details, contact the publisher at the above listed address.

Nigeria, Ghana, Sierra Leone, SA and U.S. trade bookstores and wholesalers: Please contact the Author at LASALA Writer, email: lasalawriter@yahoo.co.uk or Facebook at: https://www.facebook.com/femi.senu

Dedication

In loving memory of Elizabeth Abosede, Mary Pedetin Senu and Mama Catherine Assengone.

Contents

Acknowledgements ix
Foreword xi
Preface 3
Introduction 6
Chapter 1: The Death of Elizabeth 9
Chapter 2: Peter Goes to the City 18
Chapter 3: Life in the City 25
Chapter 4: After the Fire 31
Chapter 5: Curious at Twelve 38
Chapter 6: Peter Runs Away 43
Chapter 7: Meeting with Mary 51
Chapter 8: At Tony's Place 55
Chapter 9: THE UNEXPECTED TRUTH 62
Chapter 10: The New House boy 67
Chapter 11: My New Job 72
Chapter 12: Nowhere to Sleep 77
Chapter 13: Visit to the Village 82
Chapter 14: Cocoa Warehouse 87
Chapter 15: Run Away with a Ship 95
Message from the Author 108
My Academic Publications 110
Anticorruption Publications Online 113
Photos 117

Acknowledgements

I would like to acknowledge the assistance given to me in creating this book. While the writing of this book has involved the patience of my English tutor Trace and Melanie Baskin from Waltham Forest College, East London United Kingdom, who helped me to proof read the first five chapters. I wish to thank my twelve years old son, Josiah Senu, who stood by me. Also, special thanks to my wife who consoled me sometimes when it was difficult to continue writing. Finally, I would like to thank all those who visited my website. Their words of encouragement have strengthened me, my biggest thanks to all of you.

Foreword

Josias Senu
14. Oct, 2009

Many times over the years, I have listened to my father tell me about his experiences in Africa, about his childhood, and about the relations among the members of his family. Often he would conclude by saying that he would like, someday, to write an autobiography, and one day on the 14th of June 2007 in the afternoon he decided he would write his book. The result is a very personal story. It is the story of one man's life and ambition. It is about the family and the childhood that shaped his dreams, about the lifetime experiences that sharpened those dreams, and about the struggle to fulfil them.

On my part I hope that things turn out well and he fulfils his dream of having a proper education. The story is natural and convincing, words such as "convinced" my father thought it was "confused" but with the help of teachers, family and friends he has constructed this book from one place, his heart. Things that you think are impossible to do are made possible in this story, things that you feel are out of this world are in this world in this story, things that you think no-one can go through, the author has gone through all these things, what more could you have asked from this man?

The book in which you hold in your hands is a true life story with emotion, discipline, anger, frustration, knowledge and many more.

This book is an inspiration into the future of young ones or maybe even future generations. This book has made people cry including the author himself. Life was not great in this story but all ends well in an emotional way. The story enlightens the difficulties and hardships less privileged children or adults go through.

Everyone in this world is diverse, it means understanding that each individual is unique, and recognizing our individual differences. These can be along the dimensions of race, ethnicity, gender, socio-economic status, age, physical abilities, religious beliefs, political beliefs, or other ideologies. It is the exploration of these differences in a safe, positive, and nurturing environment. It is about understanding each other and moving beyond simple tolerance to embracing and celebrating the rich dimensions of diversity contained within each individual.

This story celebrates all the uniqueness in the world, this story celebrates that all things are possible if you put your heart and mind to it. This story is not elaborate, it is not the No.1 international bestseller, this book is about everyone from every culture, every background and every community, it shows you do not need to be from a different race, it shows you don't need to have a different skin colour, it shows you don't need to be from a different ethnic, it shows that everyone is unique and we all have one dream, one heart and one mind, and together, we can make all things possible.

This book is ultimately a nail biting story that shows how a determined man can chase his dreams until he achieves them.

Note

Josias Senu was 10 years old when I started to write this book and he wrote this foreword in 2009. Inspired by his father's determination, Josias completed an LLB in Law at the LSE in 2019 and an LLM at Harvard as a Kennedy scholar in the following year. He then completed reading for the BCL at Balliol College, Oxford. In addition, he taught Contract, Tort and Jurisprudence to undergraduate students at the LSE.

Josias is the Author of Negotiating Damages and the Compensatory Principle, published in 2019 in the Oxford Journal of Legal Studies.

THE UNEXPECTED TRUTH

Preface

Why read my book?
Direct, engaging and plain-spoken, carefully crafted, yet emotionally disarming, this book is the triumphant autobiography of a man who believes those who don't chase their dreams are guilty of cowardice. Tracing a young boy's dream into his adult years, this book inspires us all to take the leap of faith. Trawling the streets of an impoverished suburb, losing three mothers and leaving education at a young age, me Oluwafemi Senu, challenges the audacity to stand up seven times after falling six. A story of travel, traumas, hunger, desperation, romance, education and dreams, me, Oluwafemi weaves a highly entertaining, thrilling and continuously surprising autobiography. I have described myself as a slave of determination, and continues to prove that dreams can be achieved if we act on its belief. No matter our background, my message is clear: the only way we can reach tomorrow is if we keep moving today.

I was born in September 1970 in a Lagosian suburb of Nigeria. I came from a small village in Badagry, and spent most of my younger years on the streets of Lagos. Leaving Nigeria in my adolescence, I spent most of my early adult years in Gabon and Germany before moving to England in 2002.

After leaving school before I was 14, I did not have a formal basis education, though, dreamed about going to University, to fulfil a promise I had made to my aunt Mary and further my education. Five years after arriving in the UK, I began writing an autobiography about my life. I was 37 when I started. I began writing 'The Unexpected Truth' in June 2007. English was not my first language and at times it was a struggle for me to express myself accurately. At times, I even misappropriated words. Nonetheless, I persevered in my writing, determined to tell the story of my life to the world.

During this time, I also applied to numerous universities, with the aim of fulfilling my childhood dream of further education. However, my applications were continuously rejected, stating that I did not have adequate qualifications to be admitted. Realising this need, I soon applied to college, where I completed courses in Maths and English, before completing a Diploma in Law in 2009. By November 2009, I had published the first part of my autobiography, with the help of my English Tutor, Tracy and Melanie Baskin from Waltham-Forest College East London. It was an emotional period, as by this time, I had also been accepted into the University of East London —

Over recent years, I graduated from the University of East London with a degree in Criminology with Psychology and a postgraduate degree from Kingston University London, in Terrorism and Political Violence Studies. During this time, I tidied my English writing skills and certainly become more adept at expressing my thoughts. When reading over again the first part of my autobiography, this book in which you hold in your hands, I remark the huge differences in my writing then and today: "Education has truly liberated my mind."

I hope this autobiography can inspire others to embrace education positively and persevere through adversity. I hope my life experiences helps strengthen the resolve of other children, orphans and less privileged individuals out of economic hardship.

Over the course of my life, I experienced numerous trials and challenges. My experiences have shaped my outlook and the approach I takes to issues around me. I do not hail from a rich household, but the culture I inherited, the determination I showed, and the will to continue, has molded me into the person I am today.

In December 2014, I published 'A New Life', the sequel to 'The Unexpected Truth', which traces my journey from my younger to adult years. In this book, I have since the last publication reviewed its contents and a few modifications have been made in chapter 1. This chapter asks some thought-provoking questions. Buy a copy to find out why.

To my fans and lovers of my books, this is just the beginning of a new journey in my life. Why must you be a part of this? Read my first and second book, I promise, you will not be disappointed.

Introduction

Anyone that hears my experience asks if I will resolve to write about my life's account. I wasn't surprised and thought there might be many more out there that are going through similar childhood experiences I had gone through. There might also be a lot of things to learn from my account. People don't know what others normally go through until they share their experience with you. Before informing the readers about some features highlighted in this tale, allow me to tell you a tad about myself.

My name is Oluwafemi Senu, my father called me "Payoyo", a nick name he adopted from "Pius" a Baptism name given to me in Catholic Church when I was a baby. My other middle name is "Semako", this is Ogu name from Badagry Lagos Nigeria. People hardly call me "Semako." My official recognised name is Oluwafemi Senu. I was born in the city of Lagos, Nigeria, West Africa in 1970. Like any other child even though I'm now an adult, my memory lies with those children who are less privileged. This belief developed from my life history.

My story is a life time experience. The writing of this book is natural and I had made vigorous efforts to improve my education. This was because I had a less basic education when I started writing this book. The editing of the first and the second draft is my hand work and the original texts are in my words. This is a true life story that is full of emotions, laughter, discipline and much more.

I hope my story motivates young ones, gives hope to less privileged children. The story aims to encourage everyone not to give up on the challenges of life. My ambition for these objectives became vast since I discovered that I have got a story to tell. My achievement so far proved that education is possible at any age and my message to the readers is, "if you can do something good, go for it, but, if you feel you can't do it, then you are probably right." The story you are about to navigate through, is my life account. The important thing of this account, is how my life experience has helped me shaped my life. This begins after the death of Elizabeth.

After the death of Elizabeth, Mary took care of me since I was seven months old. During my childhood, I felt I was a dead man alive 'a man walking without a brain'. I am unhappy and lonely. I walked in fear, ate in fear and even slept in fear.

I went to the garbage to look for bread that was thrown away by a bakery and the left over from the garbage had been my food for days. I was facing one of the biggest challenges of my life, and it was a matter of life and death. I finally ran away with a ship to an unknown destination, my life has taught me many things and I would to share the experience with everyone. Hopefully, the story would turn someone life around too.

Note I published this book in the following order:
First version: Published by Author House-Dec. 16, 2009
Second version: Published by Blub-Nov. 16, 2014
Third version: Published by Oluwafemi Senu -Nov. 23, 2022

The third version is this book you are holding in your hands.

Thank you and I hope you will enjoy reading my book!

Chapter 1: The Death of Elizabeth

I'VE WONDERED WHY! Do you wish I wouldn't have wondered? It was so difficult for them to understand. Do you think it was difficult for me to compromise? They thought life would remain the same after death snatched the loving and caring mother away. What do you think? What impossible things could've been going through your mind right now? Strange things started to happen shortly after her death, maybe if she was alive, her children's mysterious lives would have turned to a better one, but hope is not lost. Hold on -- do you understand you've just poked me in the eye?

Her husband could have thought back to the love he used to share with his wife, if only he had thought of that? Maybe Beki could have put a stop to those wicked things she did, but who knows her motive? She could have been right? Maybe she had a point or maybe I should have taken a pain killer, but it looks like we were in a different world here. Ah, it seems I'm talking to myself, but what do you think?

Life. This world is full of unexpected things. Can you imagine all the troubles and dreadful pain that the innocent woman went through? She was a good mother, caring, and understanding but childless. She never had a child of her own, but why did she have to go through woeful things? Hmm, not just a mother but two mothers and even the third mum. She was called nasty names and was accused of vile things, people became frightened of her. Her name was Mary. She was Peter's aunt, and used to live in Akarakumo, Badagry, Lagos Nigeria. Mary had an outstanding role to play in this story. She loved children and had helped numbers of people to raise their children. She was always delightful to be in company of kids, despite her superb qualities, she was abandoned by friends and some of her family members. People were so frightened to visit her, they ran away from her. If I was there, what could I have done? Would you have run away from this woman? The childless woman died mysteriously. The cause of her death was unknown till present. People said she died of hunger, others said, she was poisoned. There was awful news circulating in the village, it was awkward, but how could people be so wicked after all she had done? If not because of her care, maybe the poor child could have died too.

How could Tony allow these terrible things to happen to his only sister? He became aware of her death, a week after her burial. In fact, I was worried and unhappy when I heard this deplorable news. I wish I could have done something about it.

I hope Mary would forgive me for all that had happened to her before my return. If only I was there, maybe I could have prevented these dejected tragedies? Are you still with me? Ok, let's get started! Mary played an important role in my life especially when I was a child. She was a good mother and her attitude inspired my life as a child. I saw how most children are privileged and are brought up in well-structured and cultured families, but some are not. Is it not true that most children are unfortunate and despondent and can't help the circumstances in which they are found? What could I have done?

Troubled, "YES"
Pathetic, "VERY"
Ghastly, "USUALLY"
Panicky, "OVER THE TOP"
Distraught, "WORDS CANNOT DESCRIBE"

Have you ever asked yourself how to live and survive these dreadful things, and to live again? Or have you ever in your life been exhorted by someone to do things that are impossible? After living again, have you had the thought to continue to live to tell your story? I can't help it not to tell this story.

In the early 70's the journey of a new born baby boy started with a tragic beginning. It was in one of the West African countries, Nigeria. The country is a place full of cultures and was blessed with lots of mineral resources and much more, people of Nigeria are friendly. Many dialects are being spoken, there are three major spoken languages; Yoruba, Awusa and Ibo. English language remains the country's official language.

In those days it happened to be a woman named Elizabeth. She got married to Tony, in March 1950. Tony was born during the First World War in December 1914. Elizabeth and her husband used to live in Lagos city, the city used to be the capital state of Nigeria. Elizabeth was a courageous, hardworking, loving, cultured and caring woman. It was told that one of her outstanding personalities was hospitality and zeal to help people in need. She was pregnant. It was sad that she couldn't make it for long after the birth of her child, which was her last pregnancy before her death. She survived by five children; Maria, Jude, Vincent, Joy and Peter. In 1970 she gave birth to a boy and the baby happened to be her last child before her death, in the middle of the year 1971. Seven months later, after giving birth,

Elizabeth died. She was seriously ill and couldn't be rescued from her illness.

My name is Peter. I've got too many things to tell you. Many years after the death of Elizabeth, I was told many things.

My father Tony, Elizabeth's husband and his junior brother Albert, carefully planned and took me to Akarakumo. The village is over twenty-one miles from the main Lagos city in Nigeria.

I was just about seven months old when it all started. Tony and Albert took a canoe, which belonged to Albert; it's not an easy task to travel to Akarakumo in those days. People living in the city had to go through lots of preparation to get prepared for a journey to a place like Akarakumo. The only easy options available for transportation in those days were pirogue and local trucks which the sides are made of wood. I went on a fifty kilometre journey away from Lagos city, where Elizabeth and Tony used to live.

I was told that I sat quietly in the middle of the pirogue. We travelled for several hours through a narrow marshy way, forest and river. The journey was dreary, devastating and lasted for about two days. Tony, Albert and I were tired. After arriving in Akarakumo, we met Tony's sister Mary. As soon as Mary perceived us, she lamented.

"YES, I knew it, I saw her, she told me, please look after him. I'm going," said Mary. Tony asked her, "What are you talking about?"

"I saw Elizabeth, in a dream. Immediately, I saw you with Peter. I knew something terrible had happened. I was having strange feelings and was worried, here you are, is it not that you've come to tell me she is dead?" replied Mary.

This was Mary's Place in Akarakumo Badagry

Mary had no child of her own; however, she now had a child to look after. Tony and Albert stayed for a few hours and later returned to Lagos may city, Tony promised to visit Mary and Peter every four weeks.

Mary was so caring; she took Peter as her own child, promised to take good care of him. She was delighted to be his career. When Peter was four years old, Mary's half-brothers brought their two daughters; Janet and Tai to live with Mary. They were playmates, keeping Peter in company. Peter was two years older than Tai and three years older than Janet. It was now five months since Tony last visited Mary and Peter, they were worried. However, at the end of the fourth week, in May, Tony visited again. Peter was happy, that Tai and Janet were brought to keep him in company.

In the year of 1976, Peter was six years old and Tony decided to take him to Lagos where he would be enrolled in primary school education.

As soon as Peter heard the news, he quickly and gently sneaked and ran away and was found eight hours later.

Mary was worried and depressed. Tony was unhappy. After what had happened, they reviewed the situation and Peter was enrolled, temporarily in a local village school, at Akarakunmo Village Badagry Lagos.

Two days after Tony's departure, Mary wanted to find out why Peter ran away, she asked, "Why did you have to run away?"

"I don't want to live with Tony, I'd like to stay with you besides, I am going to miss you," Said Peter. After a few minutes of silence, Peter asked,

"Why can't you come with us?" He wouldn't give Mary a chance to speak,

"Hence he is your husband, and by the way, why are both of you not staying together?"

Mary wasn't cheerful and kept silent for some few minutes. She lacked immediate response to those questions because they were hard questions for her to answer.

Peter had never been told that Mary was not his biological mother. Mary was totally confused and quickly said without taking note of herself, "Oh my God, the boy is about to find out the mystery of his mother's death." However, she continued to ask herself the following questions. "Should I

wait for Tony to come or tell him the truth myself? Is it the right time for him to know that I am not his biological mother?"

Peter's mother died when he was just seven months old, if he is aware that Mary is not his biological mother, what would happen to the love they both shared. Peter thought Mary was Tony's wife but she was not. Tony and Mary are brother and sister. He even thought, Tai and Janet were his biological sisters. What a mystery?

"What should I do to sort out these mysteries?" asked Mary.

She was confused, what could you have done? Hmm, what is going through your mind right now? Be patient, you are soon to discover the mystery!

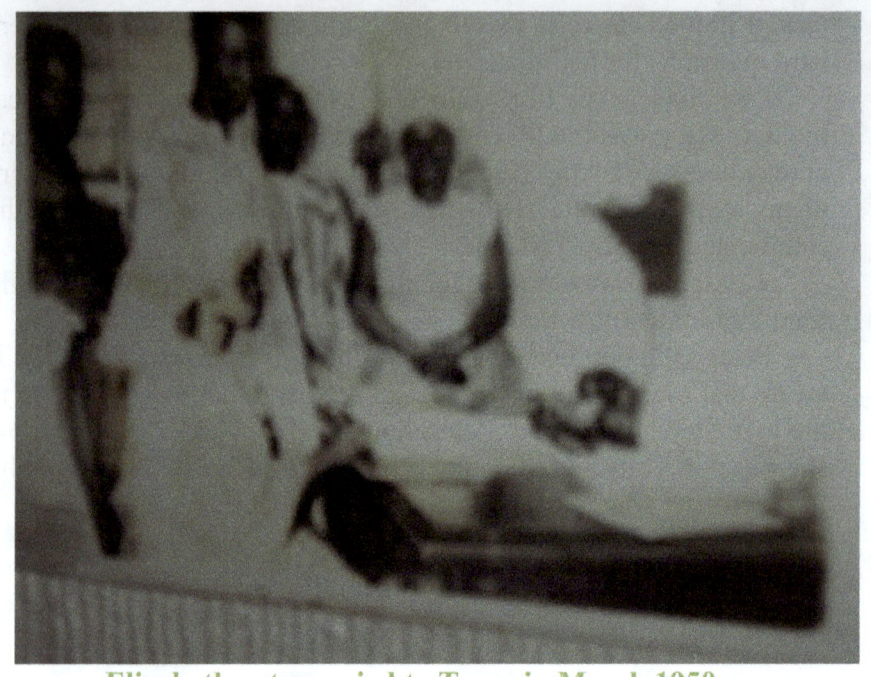

Elizabeth got married to Tony, in March 1950

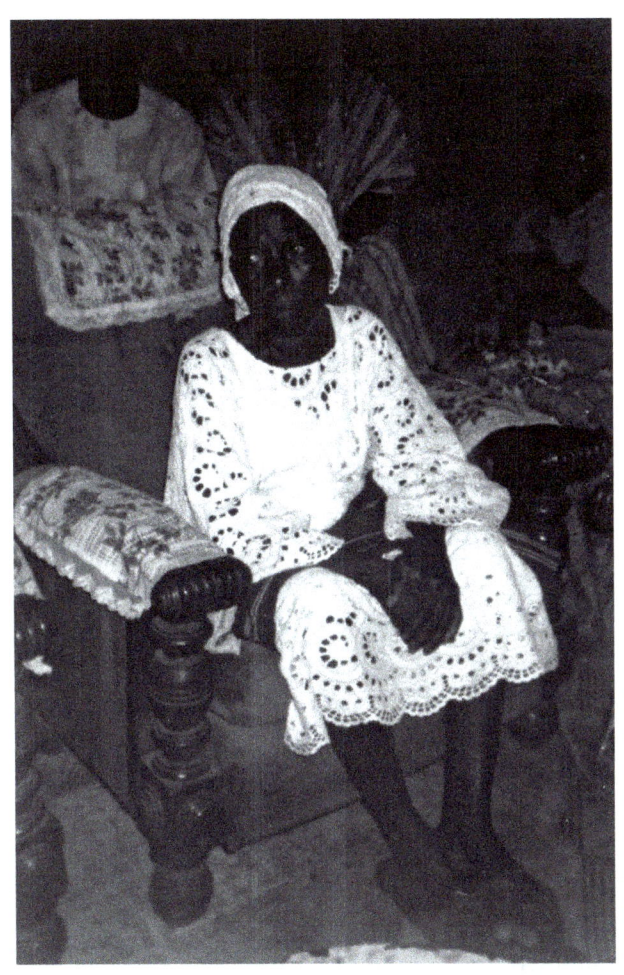
Mama Mary Pedetin Senu, Peter Aunt

Chapter 2: Peter Goes to the City

Mary was as brave as a lion and was good as gold. She taught Peter how to cope and endure hardships. Sometimes she would take him to the farm, and sometimes they were accompanied by Janet's father. Mary had an uncle; her uncle's grandson' name was Bino. He was two years older than Peter.

Bino and his parents lived opposite Mary's house. Bino, would sometimes, play with Peter and sometimes go to the farm together. Bino became Peter's childhood friend.

In Akarakunmo, there was a river that ran through to the other side where the sea is located. People from the village, would normally come to the river in groups to cut straw.

A canoe would pick a group of eight or twelve women, to the other side of the river, to cut the straw.

The women would hold a short machete or a dagger and cut underneath the straw, after they'd finished cutting the straw, which weighed about seventy kilograms each, they would put it on their heads. The straw was wrapped together first, the women would wait for the canoe, and then the straw would be loaded. The women would travel back again to where they met in a group. The straw would be divided into two parts; the farm owner would take one part and give the other part to the women.

The women would take their part of straw to about two to three kilometres away from the river. The straw would be dried in the sun, after the straw had finished drying, it would be taken to about three kilometres away to weave.

The straw is weaved with thread and later bounded together.

Tai and Janet were experts in this exercise; they had been trained for this job. They could weave incredibly fast. When they had finished weaving, Tai used to boil water and add colouring. Afterwards, the straw would be decorated.

The people would have finished preparation of the straw, which was now transformed into a mat before the market day, every week. The mat and some un-weaved straw would be transported through public transport or by canoe. When the weaved straw, and the un-weaved straw arrived at the Badagry market, it was neatly presented. The market is the second largest market in Lagos. People would come from Lagos city to purchase them. After the day's sales Mary would use the money to buy food and kept some money for Tai, Janet and Peter. The money kept would be used to pay for their school fees. The straw business, this is the Badagry women tradition and that was one of the only jobs available to them in those days. The straw was used to make mats.

One day, Tony visited Peter, when he was about to leave, Peter approached him and said.

"Dad, I will follow you to the city, but you have to promise, that Mary is coming with us," Peter loved Mary so dearly and would not like to miss her for a second, but there were still lots more things to that. He then decided to find out.

"Why is it that you and mum are not living together?" asked Peter.

Meanwhile, Mary had already explained everything to Tony, about the inquisitiveness of Peter's questions. Not again! What is Tony going to tell Peter now?

Soon Peter would be seven years old and the more his age advanced, the more curious he became. After a while, Tony replied, "My son, your mother and I had previously decided that you stay in the village, we also agreed that, you had to come with me to Lagos. In turn, your mother will visit you every fourth week of each month, just as I used to do." Hearing that, Peter lamented, "No Dad, I want my mum to stay with us permanently in the city, not to visit us every fourth week of each month." Peter wasn't happy and was troubled and wouldn't like to go alone to the city without Mary. He asked again,

"One more thing Dad, are Tai and Janet coming to the city with us?"

"No Peter, Tai and Janet will stay behind in the village," replied Tony.

"No Dad, I want Tai and Janet to come with us. PLEASE," Peter begged.

Tony kept quiet, thinking and was depressed. However, Mary was watching and wanted the conversation to end well, "My God, please help me out of this misery," said Mary.

Peter, is about to find out the mysteries surrounding his mother's death. The situation is unclear to him, Peter thought, that Mary was Tony's wife and Tony was confused too and didn't know how to get out of these troubles. "Peter thinks Mary; my sister is my wife. I think this is the time I had to let the cat out of the bag, but hold on a minute, coming to think about it, what would Peter's reaction be? No, I have to tell him that Mary is not his biological mother and that he's mother died when he was seven months old," thought Tony.

Tony was so frustrated, as he was about to let the cat out of the bag, Mary rushed in,

"Stop Tony, we both know what you are going to say."

As she looked into Peter's eyes, it was too emotional. Tears fell out from her eyes and she said "Peter, I will go with you to the city, I will stay there with you and stand by you. Tony is your father, soon both of us will live together," said Mary.

"Mum, don't cry. I am happy, that you will come to the city with us," said Peter.

Phew! What a relief for Tony. He laughed loudly saying.

"Thank-you Mary, I was just confused too. Peter makes me remember Elizabeth," said Tony.

"Who is Elizabeth, Dad?" asked Peter.

"Oh, sorry Peter, she was one of my sisters," replied Tony. What a slip of tongue!

Peter and Mary would soon be relocated to the city, what happened to Tai and Janet? Previously, Tony and Mary had concluded

in private, that Mary would be moving temporarily to the city with Peter. After staying with him in the city for a period of one month, Mary would return to the village. Afterwards, Mary would be visiting again, in every fourth week of each month.

Meanwhile, arrangements had been made for Tai and Janet to stay with Mary's half-brothers, while Mary would be away in the city. Hmm...Will Peter support their decision?

Soon afterwards, Tony departed to the city. A few weeks after his departure, he revisited the village again. Tony stayed in the village for a whole week. Mary and Peter were given enough time to get prepared for the journey. The three of them, including Tony, would soon start to make a journey to the city. It was said that Peter was such a nice boy in the village and the villagers would soon miss him.

Before the end of that same week, the village people organised a surprise leaving party for him. Peter was so happy but sad at the same time because Tai and Janet would be left behind. He liked them so much and wouldn't like to miss them.

This is Mile 2 -The Road to Badagry

Elizabeth with Tony in 1950s

Chapter 3: Life in the City

In the beginning of 1977, Mary and Peter moved to the city and soon after he met Vincent and Joy. He had already met them before during one of their holiday visits to the village so they weren't strangers to him. Vincent had been formerly introduced to him as his brother and Joy as his sister who lived in the city. They stayed with Tony while he stayed in the village with Mary.

Tony was amongst the middle class group during his middle age and lived in a house owned by him. His lounge was narrow and long and there was a door towards the end part of it. Beside the door, just at the immediate right there was a lobby. The lobby would soon be my room. It was a nice place and was not far away from where Tony's room was situated. Vincent and Joy's rooms weren't far away either.

Vincent was four years older than Peter and Joy was two years older than him. He didn't know what their characters were but would soon get acquainted with them.

It wasn't so long when he started his education, the city life was so rough and he was like a "JJC" meaning JOHNNY JUST COME. You must have your eyes wide open to live in a city like Lagos.

It was hard for him to cope with school life. The funniest thing was that, he started becoming a baby again. On his first day in the class, he was expecting Mary to attend class with him and refused to stay in the class unless Mary came in with him. In the class, when Mary was about to leave, he asked her, "Where are you going mum?"

She replied "I'm going home"

He then quickly said, "No mum, I'm coming with you." He was disturbing the whole class. Mary had no choice but had to wait till the end of the session. This was an ongoing problem that continued for almost about two months. Mary became ill and blamed Tony for bringing Peter to the city. He was very sorry for her illness and said

"Mum I'm sorry, I thought you'd leave me at the school and return back to the village without me."

He started getting used to the city life and Mary was well again but she decided to rent a shop to sell accessories beside his school and Mary could manage the City and the village life.

One day in the beginning of 1978 Tony and Mary had a gathering that Tony should get another wife to help ease the tension at home. It had been top secret of the family not to make it clear to Peter that Mary wasn't his biological mother. Before the end of that same year, Tony got married to another woman named Beki and soon Mary would limit her journeys to the city. Would Peter cope with Beki? That is one question that never got away from Mary's head. Mary hugged Peter saying, with tears running down her cheeks, "I will miss you but I promise to see you as soon as I can."

The hug continued for about three minutes. Soon afterwards they separated but not for long. With all that was happening around him, he started to realise the important role of a mother in someone's life and he thought missing Mary for too long would be like missing the whole world. Would he get the kind of moral support, just as Mary used to do, from Beki?

I was eight years old when it all started. Tony gave more attention to Vincent, Joy and I, claimed Beki.

Vincent was twelve years old; Joy was ten and Peter was eight. Vincent and Joy attended classes in the afternoon and he attended classes in the morning, both Vincent and Joy were capable to cope with the strain and strike Beki was about to begin. It all started like a wisecrack.

One day when I arrived home from school.

"You come here! Why are you late today?" Beki asked.

"Good- afternoon Mother," Peter replied.

"What is good about the afternoon, don't call me mum, I am not your mother and I am not the one that killed your mama" said Beki. I was shocked hearing what she just said and quickly replied.

"Kill my mum? My mum is not dead; my mum is in the village."

Hearing this Beki was hateful to me and threw me to the floor and knocked my head on the ground. I was confounded. She flogged me repeatedly and gave me stringent instructions while I bled at the front of my head.

After a few seconds I fainted and later found myself at a local hospital, when I regained my consciousness, Beki and Tony were already sitting by my bed side. As I was about to explain what'd happened, Tony explained, "Beki said, you fell and knocked your head on the floor." I was confused as Beki stared at me with scary eyes. I was shaking and panicked. For the first time in my life I felt like an abandoned child. In the late evening of that same day I approached Tony, "Dad, was my mother killed?" asked Peter

"No Peter, why did you ask?" Replied Tony

"Beki said that she was not the one who killed my mother, I told her my mother was not dead, she was in the village," replied Peter.

As I was about to continue, Beki appeared from nowhere and interrupted our conversation.

"I'm sorry Tony it's a slip of the tongue I never meant to. I meant his real mother is in the village." Beki said quickly. Tony kept silent for a couple of seconds before he replied by saying.

"Come here my son, your mother is Mary and she's in the village and soon she will visit you again, as promised."

Not so long after the incident, Beki became pregnant and later gave birth to Vero my half-sister. Two weeks before Vero's birth, Beki invited her mother to come and spend some time with us in the city. It had been previously arranged, that her mother would help her look after her first child after her birth. Two weeks after Vero's birth a terrible thing happened.

On that day, I came back from school it was in the afternoon at the end of the year 1978. I was sleeping in my room and there was a fire outbreak in the city, just ten metres away from our house.

The fire was too dreadful to bear. The people in the area were running for their lives and looking for refuge. I was still sleeping in my room, the whole place had turned into a horrific night and there was darkness everywhere. The fire came through my door and the immediate door towards the fire exit.

The flames of the fire and the heat were surrounding my bed. The heat was too much and was very hot. I woke up and found out that I had already been caught up in the middle of the fire. By my right was a window, fitted with burglar proof rails. I was frightened and confused; I didn't know what to do. I thought, I was going to die in the fire but however put my hand through the rails and knocked on the window hoping to receive help. As I continued knocking, I could also see the fire approaching. I was scared and shouted for help, but wondered if anyone could hear me.

"Help, can anyone help me, help please God help me anybody help," the situation was emotional and I felt sorry for myself, I was crying and helpless and I thought this, would be the end of my life. After a few seconds, I heard a voice saying, "If you can hear me, move away from the window." The voice heard was a stranger's voice and I was imagining who that might be, but I replied, "I can't move away, there is fire everywhere in my room."

I was then thrown to the bed with the heavy force of the fire men's water hose. I was rescued by the fire men and was taken to paramedics for medical treatment. It was now late in the evening. I was taken to rejoin Beki and her mother with Vero where they had taken refuge. As soon as Beki took sight of me, her veins swelled up around her neck, she became wrathful and was marching towards me like a lion looking for someone to devour. She shouted, "WHERE HAVE YOU BEEN PETER?" I was afraid and quickly said, "I was in my room sleeping." Hearing that she became furious, "No, we searched for you everywhere, you were nowhere to be found," Beki argued back.

I was still with two of the firemen at that time, hearing what she had said, one of the men intervened on my behalf, "No, we rescued Peter, through a broken window in his room." Hearing what the men has just said, she was confused in words, "Oh," Beki grunted. The fireman handed me over to Beki and I was taken to refuge.

Vincent and Joy came back from school and joined us in the same refugee camp. It was one of the saddest moments of my life, all of us were dispirited. A few minutes later, Tony came back from work and found out what had happened. His three houses, his cars, his possessions, his money and provision shop had been destroyed by the fire. He cried in horror and shouted repeatedly, "GOD, WHY," It was the first time I saw Tony cry.

There were lots of other people's properties that were destroyed too, that area of landscape was full of horror and people were grouchy. There was a neighbour living about twelve metres away from where the disaster took place, people called her Mama Yemisi. Tony's property was completely destroyed by the fire, but Mama Yemisi's property was not affected by it. She gave us a room to live in. The room was about three metres long and four metres wide; we lived there for about one year. The room was congested, because seven of us had to share it. We lived in the apartment for over a period of one year, during that period, Mary visited us but not as frequently as she used to do. Our current situation was pathetic and we were in need of helpful hands.

In the end of the year 1979, Vincent had to leave us and live with Tony's friend Baba Kushalu. Baba Kushalu lived in the city, just about six kilometres away from us, our condition was so poor that Vincent had to drop out of school meanwhile, Joy and I continued our education.

Three square meals per day, wasn't any longer our priority. We ate one meal per day which was in the evening. Sometimes neighbours gave us food to eat. This had sustained us for several months. The situation continued and prompted Beki's mother to return back to her home town, that won't change Beki's attitude towards us. Terrible things happened just after her return, what could that be?

Peter Positioned on the left-Tony in the Middle-Vincent in the back-Joy on the Right

Chapter 4: After the Fire

Life after the fire nightmare; during the fire incident, the water pipes that supplied water where we lived had been destroyed by the fire. It was difficult to get water for our daily use. The only place currently available to fetch water was far away and was about two kilometres from where we lived. We had about four big drums to fill water in every day. After filling up to three drums, Beki would throw one away to make it two more drums to be filled up. After completing the fourth drum, she would throw another drum away to make it one more drum to be filled up. That had been her game for several months.

She made life miserable for Joy and I, we were so frightened of her. We couldn't report her neither her attitude towards us, to Tony. The situation persisted for a longer period.

Life was so dreadful and was not the same after the fire incident. It wasn't long again when Tony built a self-contained apartment. The apartment was built with zincs and the zincs were used to surround the sides and the roofing. Some of the zinc was collected from the remains of the burnt house building where the fire burnt down. The apartment was built with the help and voluntary contributions of Tony's friends. Soon after completion of the apartment, Tony and his entire household including myself moved into the new apartment. I had always hoped that, the new environment would bring a change to Joy and my situation however, my aspiration was wrong, hmm. Do you know what happened to me next?

In the beginning of 1980, Beki got pregnant again and gave birth to Larry; soon Beki's mother returned to the city to join us again and that was shortly after John's birth. She stayed with us for a longer period. Her presence didn't make any difference at home but rather, it made things worse.

Joy and I were being maltreated. Sometimes we were beaten by Beki and her mother and starved by them. Tony didn't care about us and used to show more attention to Beki. He believed everything she said. Food wasn't our major concern as we have been used to starvation. Beki gave us very little food. Joy got a bigger portion of food than mine, and would usually exchange her food for mine.

One day Mary visited us and was so sad to find out what we had been going through at the hands of Beki. We explained everything that had happened. Beki denied the facts and Tony took sides with her, the situation at home worsened after Mary became knowledgeable of our problem.

Mary was unhappy, she left the city and was very annoyed. She vowed that she would come back soon to take Joy and I to the village.

After Mary left for the village, I started thinking and was asking myself, "Would Tony allow Mary to take us to the village?" I also thought that, this might be a good opportunity for me to be closer to Mary because I knew she had got a lot to tell me maybe, she was hiding a secret from me. After some time, things got back to normal but that didn't still change Beki's attitude towards us.

In 1981 I was now eleven years old and something was going on through my mind, I was troubled. I felt like a condemned child and I wanted to run away from home it's like my world was falling apart and all the debris was falling on me. I thought there was no one to talk to or care about me, someone to share things with or that would show parental affection towards me.

Mary was still in the village. Tony that used to care for me didn't care anymore and Tony's wife Beki has made me a stranger in the home. I was missing Mary so much and was thinking on what to do. I was upset and confused, my situation was worrying as a child and I was desperately in need for help.

I became very frightened and needed someone to talk to. I then started saying to myself "Oh my God, should I run away from home? Where is Mary?"

I had previously made it known while I was still in the village. I remembered, I told Mary that, I wouldn't want to come to the city but she wouldn't listen to me.

I was thinking of a possible solution to my problem and I thought I knew what to do.

I thought the best thing to do was to run away from home, yes, I will run away and then, go to the village, there, I will stay with Mary, I thought. But I needed money for my transport, but where was I going to find money? I became worried again and wanted to find solutions for myself, Hmm. Yes, I thought it would be helpful to steal money from Tony's wardrobe but how? I remembered that Mary would used to tell me, "Never take anything that does not belong to you, if you take it against the person's will, it is called stealing," but I was desperate and needed to do something about my journey, my heart was troubled. I thought, it was the right thing to do and didn't think this was wrong besides, Tony hates us because if he doesn't, why is it that he always takes sides with Beki. I was fed up and didn't want to stay in Tony's place any longer. Would Joy support my plans? After having thought about the matter I thought, I would tell Joy about it. I was in haste and rushed towards her, "Hi Joy."

"Hi Peter" replied Joy. I then quickly said to her.

"I was thinking of running away from home, I thought I will go back to the village to stay with Mary, I know Tony doesn't like us anymore." Hearing what I had said, she was sad and responded, "No Peter, you can't run away."

She thought it would be wrong for me to run away from home and wouldn't want anything bad to happen to me on the way to the village. I wouldn't listen to my sister and insisted, nothing would happen to me, I would be fine.

After hearing that, Joy was troubled and wanted to do everything in her power to prevent me not to runaway. She said in a modulation tone, "Besides you don't have money for transport and I will miss you," afterwards Joy asked me a question.

"Have you thought about what would happen to your education?"

I knew Joy was right, but couldn't help it. I also knew Beki hated us too, maybe she was jealous because of the love and affection that Tony previously gave to us and she had succeeded to take that love away from us. Without hesitation, my ambitions became uncontrolled and my emotions became clear, it's obvious what my next action would be, consequently I decided to leave home. Afterwards, I said to Joy, "I've got to go I know nothing is going to happen to me," said Peter.

It wasn't clear where I would get transport fees which would enable me to make the journey to the village but later decided to take some money from Tony's wardrobe. I knew exactly where Tony normally kept his money but I was worried what the outcome would be if he found out about it.

Joy was unhappy with what I was about to do and was crying because she knew that she wasn't going to see me for a while. We both held hands for a while, I was sad too and I put my hands across her shoulder and tried to console her not to cry again. I found myself crying too and we now consoled each other, it was an emotional moment of my life because, I wasn't going to see her for a while too.

Five days later, I ran away from home, I knew everyone would be worried and perhaps looking for me. I was scared and didn't know where to go and thought it would be good idea to go to the village. I also thought going to the village straight away might cause me another problem, may be Joy would be pressurised and would tell Tony where I was and Tony would come looking for me. I knew it wouldn't be easy because Mary would be under pressure too and she would take me back to the city. "My God, this would be too much for me to bear what should I do now," I was thinking of another alternative way to go about this matter. I then asked myself this question, could I have done anything different in this situation?

I was troubled and was confused. I didn't know where to go, I thought I would go to the next city or town maybe, anywhere or anyplace. My problem was that, I just wanted to get away from Beki and Tony. After contemplating what to do, I later went to the next town which was about five kilometres away.

The town's name was called Olokodana this was one of Lagos's popular towns and there was a field alongside the high street. Soon I would be wandering around in the streets. My first night in Olokodana high street was pathetic. As the night fell, I was worried of where to sleep however, I found an abandoned vehicle which was parked nearby Olokodana's high street and the vehicle was close to the field. The vehicle became my shelter for a period of time. I begged in the street, my clothes were dirty and stank. Passers-by thought I was a deranged person living in an abandoned vehicle. I was depressed and didn't know what to do or neither any other way out of my predicament. My life was totally wretched. I felt like dying and I became slow in my stepping, my heart was weak and my body became empty. I felt like going to the village to see Mary but I wasn't sure of doing that. I pitied her for all that she'd gone through because of me; I was anxious and concerned if I would die soon.

One day while wandering about the street, I saw a man walking towards me. I was scared and thought something bad would happen if he approached me because he looked anxious in the way he walked. It had been days that I ran away from home and I knew by now people would have been looking for me. As the man's steps became intensive, I was nervous and immediately and quickly ran. The man ran after me but I was faster than him, he pursued me and I got very tired, he grasped the back of my shirt and apprehended me. I kept bawling for help, people came around us and the man had to explain in details the reasons behind his chase. The people wouldn't let him go with me, however, he said to them, "He has been missing from home for the past month."

Unmistakably, I then knew that the stranger might have been sent by Tony and he was there to take me home. I was worried and afraid and wouldn't go with him, "No I don't want to go with you, please don't take me home," I was crying and refused to go with him.

One passer-by said. "I usually see him around; he normally sleeps in an abandoned vehicle across the street. We thought he was a mad person"

After hearing what the passer-by said, the stranger held me tight and I was then taken home. The man dragged me quickly through the streets while people were looking at us; I was troubled because I knew that there were fateful days ahead of me. On arriving home we met Joy and Tony. Joy was crying and Tony gave me a horrible look and asked the man to take me to Albert's house. Albert was a junior brother to Tony; he lived three streets away from Tony's place. When we arrived at Albert's home he welcomed the stranger but pushed me against the wall with a muscular smack… I thought I was dreaming, he shoved me to the floor and hauled me back up then he smacked me again. His blow was like a thunder strike and I was temporarily blinded. He locked the door behind himself and asked me to remove my clothes. I was stripped down by him, Albert pushed me and I fell to the table in his living room. He took a blade and cut me several times in the back.

The cut was about two to three centimetres away from each other.

He took some pepper and spread it all over the bleeding back and whipped it vigorously. I was in pain and helpless. He whipped me many times. I was shouting and crying I was in a terrifying situation all I wished for at that moment was death. Albert's wife was outside pleading on my behalf too, "Albert leave the poor boy alone, please Albert don't kill him," said Ana Albert's wife.

I remembered Ana was banging on Albert's door crying and saying "I hope you remember the mystery surrounding his childhood."

On hearing what Ana had just said, Albert stopped beating me. I was in agony and was taken home, when I got home I saw how pleased Tony and his wife were, the smiles in their faces were tremendous. After carefully noticing the cuts on my body and the extent of my wounds, Tony became furious and was uncomfortable to look into my eyes. At that point I was nervous and didn't know what to do. Joy was crying, I was crying too. Mary became aware of the harsh treatment I had gone through and she arrived in the city before the night fell of the next day.

Immediately after her arrival, she was not happy with the horrible treatment I had gone through. She was so angry with Tony. Her noise was circulating around the whole place and the argument was intensified. I was afraid and wouldn't want the problem to escalate. The situation at home was devastating. Everyone was so sad and tempered. This had been ongoing for a while since Mary's arrival from the village and she decided not to return so soon. Mary promised to stay for some time. It was like a cat and mouse game between Mary, Albert, Tony and Beki because Mary wouldn't allow anything to go wrong with me again, not after the things I had just experienced.

Aftermath, I was ill and couldn't attend school for over three months but something kept occurring to me and I would soon be desperate to find an answer to my worrying question. What could that be? I remembered this statement during my ordeal with Albert, "I hope you remember the mystery surrounding his childhood." Said Ana Albert's wife.

Mystery surrounding my childhood, what did she mean by saying that? I thought there should be lots to Ana's statements and I started reading meanings into it. I was anxious about those words and was convinced that, Mary had a lot questions to answer but, how was I going to go about it? The situation surrounding these mysteries was not clear to me and I couldn't really figure out what it's all about. I was in the dark from my entire family and sometimes got worried and confused either to place Mary as Tony's wife or Tony's sister. Do you know what happened next? This was interesting!

Chapter 5: Curious at Twelve

I was now twelve years old and Mary was still staying with us in the city, sometimes she had to travel to the village to see Tai and Janet. At Tony's place, things didn't get better at home. The tension at home was immense and Beki thought Mary had become the policewoman of the home. I and Mary were so close and she had also become my protector. One day I asked Mary questions in an inquisitive way.

"Good morning mum," I said. The manner I greeted Mary was amusing and was different from every other day, Mary looked into my eyes. Immediately she knew there must be something behind my mood.

"Good morning Peter, how was your night," she replied.

"Not so good," replied Peter.

"Not so good, but why Peter?" Asked Mary. She was concerned and wanted to know why my night was bad. She pulled me gently to her, while I was sitting on her laps, she asked me in a lonely voice, "What is it my son." After seeing Mary's gesture, without hesitation, I said quickly, "I heard, Ana Albert's wife telling Albert to remember the mystery surrounding my childhood." After hearing what I had just said she became furious and wanted to know more and she asked me series of questions.

"Mystery, how, when and why?" I was concerned of her nervousness and it was interesting to me that, why would she be nervous? Before I could reply and as she was about to ask me another question, I replied... "It's when Albert was beating me."

Only God knows what was going on in her mind. The expression of her face could tell me that something was wrong somewhere. Mary said quickly, "Listen son, you are a wonderful boy and we all love you." She made me understand that probably, the reasons behind Ana's statement... "Mystery surrounding my child hood" was to stop Albert from hurting him. Come to think about it, how long can they continue to fool me? I was suspicious of their actions, in particular Mary's behaviour. I thought she said things just to please me or maybe to prevent me from asking further questions, however I wouldn't be stopped and I still wanted to know more. I asked again, "But, why mum?" Mary was someone that gets panicked quickly and sheds tears when things are uncontrollable, but how was she going to handle this matter? She was panicked and said quickly, "I don't know." Immediately she replied, she fell into heavy tears and was crying for several minutes, she looked uncontrollable. I couldn't help it and burst into tears too. The mood was emotionally bad, it was sad seeing her crying but I still wondered why she had to cry because of the questions I asked. This was just the beginning; however, I still had many more questions to ask but decided to leave it for another opportunity. But how long could I wait before raising another question? Or how long could you have waited to clear the air if you were in my situation?

Two weeks after, it was very early in the morning of that day. I woke Mary from her sleep. What could be the motive behind this? I raised another issue, "Why is it that, since you have been staying in the city, hardly you spend time with Tony?" Peter asked.

Mary had been staying in the city but off and on between the city and the village for some time now, however, while in the city, I expected Mary and Tony to sometimes stay together, eat together and perhaps sleep together, just the way husband and wife does. I hadn't seen that and wanted to know why. Could you have thought the same way? How Mary would handle this fresh conversation, is what I was yet to find out and I thought there were lots to it.

Mary couldn't figure out what my inquisitiveness was all about or may lead to, but was conscious in selection of her words. She expressed her feeling and said that Tony has been staying in the city without her and staying in the village without him didn't bother her either. He had Beki, "anyway," said Mary.

I was adamant and would not be allowed to be persuaded or be deceived again, hearing what Mary just said, I asked, "Does that mean that Tony doesn't love you, because he has got Beki?"

Mary should have heard enough of me by now. Did that mean that, she would give in to my pressure? Without hesitation, she replied "No Peter, we love each other however I am here because of you."

"Because of me?" asked Peter. Noticing that I would not cease from throwing questions at her, she was uncomfortable. Her eyes were like a heavy cloud that was ready to pour rain from the sky. I was not happy too but however quickly changed the conversation. From then on, I began having sensations that something was wrong somewhere.

I kept imagining what that could be, but I had no clue or nil knowledge, that Mary wasn't my biological Mother. In fact, there weren't any indications that my biological mother had died a long time ago. Apart from the worrying questions that troubled me, there were still cat and mouse games between Beki and me. I was pressurised with lots of mysteries happening to me, "It's true." I was being fed up and overstressed with the maltreatment of Beki my father's wife, who should also be a caring stepmother but had turned against me. Her cruel attitude was shown in the way she treated me, she would sometimes deny Joy and I food and also overlabour us. Beki pretended to be doing well towards us, especially when she saw Tony and Mary around us, but would maltreat us when they were away. Tony loved Beki so much and would believe anything she said against us. Joy and I were helpless. Mary was aware of Beki's tricks, but was conscious with the way and manner she dealt with both Beki and Tony. But how long would she play it cool with them?

Mary was running out of patience and would spend some of her time with us to prevent Beki's malice. Tony was furious with the events surrounding him and he was threatening to send Mary to the village. His furiousness became intensive and he got involved in an argument that took place between Mary his sister and Beki. Mary was in support of Joy and I and would do all she could to protect us from Beki's maltreatment. It was so bad at home, while all this was going on, amongst the questions that kept coming to my mind was, why am I being so maltreated by Tony and Beki? Was this the way children were being treated in their families? Why was I being treated in such way? Is it a terrible upbringing?

These questions were so worrying for me as a child and I used to think, why is it that my life and upbringing was so different from other children.

While I was thinking of these things, I immediately found out that I was speaking to myself. I used to ask myself this question, "Who else was in my kind of situation?"

I was lonely and thought God didn't even exist because if he did, why were there so many bad things happening around me?

I used to have these strange feelings that something terrible would soon happen to me and was always scared. I was so frightened to stay or move closer to Beki and Tony. The worst thing was that, I started seeing Beki as an evil woman and Tony as the agent and husband of evil. I used to cry always and my tears had turned to a serious pain.

One day, Tony just arrived from a week's journey. I complained to him that, for the past two days I had not eaten and that Beki had refused to give me food. Tony turned around and hit me hard and then tied my hand to the back with a rope. He put me in a drum and rolled me on the floor then took me out and beat me several times, I then cried in horror. I was thinking that, maybe he was not my father. I cried and cried in horror several times. Joy was crying too and quickly ran to call for help.

Ana, Albert's wife, came. She pleaded on my behalf and I was free from Tony.

Mary had always been there to protect me but it was unfortunate that she had to go to the village for an emergency. She left the city just three days before Tony's arrival. When she arrived the damage had been done to me, there was a terrible fight between Tony and Mary. She vowed not to stay away from me again. But how long would this last?

I loved Mary so much and all she was going through because of me. These were too much to bear. I had always hoped that, she would be rewarded abundantly for all she had done for me.

Nevertheless, I was positive with my actions and I was well aware that good things were good and bad things were evil. I also have these strong feelings that all shall be well and would be free from my predicament one day but I can't explain why I am so hated by Beki.

Since the fire outbreak in 1978 things weren't the same for Tony he had become a poor man and most of his property and wealth has been lost in the fire incident. We had to go through lots of hardship to survive, Joy and I used to sell bath soap, washing soap on high streets. The goods were usually put on our heads and were heavy to bear for longer period. Because of overlabour and pressure we were undergoing, Joy and I had less time to concentrate on our education.

I was now thirteen years old and Joy was fifteen years. I attended a local boy's secondary school which was about three miles from where we lived. Mary had always been there for me. Sometimes she would spend much of her time in the village to work in order to get some money to assist my education. It was so difficult for her to manage the city and the village life.

Chapter 6: Peter Runs Away

Peter was about fourteen years old now and he was in year nine. His education life was poor and he wasn't doing well at school, the time was so hard and it was difficult for him to cope with school life and he had to drop out of school, before then something terrible happened. What could that be?

One day, it was in the evening, Mary called him, "My son, you're over thirteen years old, I know it has been difficult for you to cope with Beki." He thought that was all she had to say but the story was so greater than what he thought. "Joy will be sixteen years old soon and both of you should start to learn how to look after each other," she was hoping to go to the village to do some farming so that she would help to ease the problem at home and support their education. Come to think of what she'd said and with the look of things, it was clear that she would be leaving them soon however, Peter said, "Mum, it's okay by me but I know Beki will continue to do terrible things to us." After hearing what he said, she replied "Son, I won't be long to see you and Joy and I know, Albert's wife, Ana, loves you so much, I have spoken to her to keep watch over you."

At this point Peter had no choice and thought he must learn to get used to his misfortune without Mary being there at all times. Ana was invited by Mary that same night and both of them had a conversation at length. Mary said, "Ana, I know you are of a good character, please look after these children for me, I won't be long, I just have to go to the village" Mary told Ana that she needed to work in her farm so that she would make some money to help support their education. Ana also told Joy and Peter what to do in case Beki starts her hostile attitudes. "Listen Joy, this is what you should do, anytime that Tony and Beki start to maltreat Peter, run quickly and call me and Peter you do the same for Joy," said Ana. They were so happy for Ana's supports and both Joy and Peter responded, "Okay Ana." Ana and Albert lived a mile away from Tony's home.

A week after Mary left for the village, things started to happen again. As predicted, Beki wouldn't change her attitude towards them. Meanwhile, it was still a challenge for Peter to cope with education. Tony showed more interest in Joy's education than Peter'.

He always complained that Peter's school results were so bad and he would show more attention checking Joy's school results and often ignored Peter'.

A few months later, during the month of June 1984, Peter was still at fourteen, he arrived from school, and was hungry. Beki gave him a small plate of food and gave the larger portion to her daughter Vero. She gave Joy a plate of food too. Joy's portion was a little bigger than Peter'.

After a while, Beki left them in the dining room. Joy swapped her bigger portion for Peter' she always did that anyway. A few minutes later Beki came in with sand in her hand. She poured the sand into Peter's food. He was so sad and was crying. Joy was crying too. Beki took a cane and whipped Peter. Joy was whipped too. She warned her never to swap her food for Peter again. Peter was frustrated and felt he was about to go mad and immediately ran outside to about eight metres distance away from where Beki was standing. He picked a flat stick and wanted to hurt Beki for all the bad things she had done to him. He threw the stick at her, but Joy quickly ran to the front of Beki and covered her with her body. He could remember saying, "Get out of the way Joy."

She didn't listen to him and Peter threw the stick, the stick hit Joy's tummy. Meanwhile, Beki was about seven months pregnant. He was sad that Joy was hurt by the stick but at the same time was happy that it didn't hit Beki's big tummy. He didn't regret his actions anyway.

Hmm, he definitely knew that there would be fire on the mountain when Tony came back! He was scared and didn't know what to do but thought it would be good to run away. He quickly sneaked and ran away before Tony came back from work. A few hours later Peter was told by friends that police were looking for him, two days later, two police men arrested him. He was so scared and panicked when the Lagos police approached him, "Hey boy, come here." They said, his father asked them to arrest him,

"But why?" asked Peter.

"Don't ask us why," replied the police men." They also told him, Tony said, they can keep him for as long as they wish. Peter was taken to a local police station. At the police station, the police said they were sorry and had no option than to do what his father had instructed them to do. He was given three lashes of cane. Afterwards, one of the officers came in and said, "Leave the poor boy alone, keep him as his father has instructed." The police officer gave him food and instructed the rest of his colleagues "Be sure he has some sense of freedom and release him afterwards." The officer was so kind to him, Peter thought he must be a higher ranking officer. He blamed the other officers for their hostile behaviour towards him.

Peter was disappointed in Tony's behaviour in the way and manner he handled his matter. He hated him for what he did and had no affection for him either. At that point, "I felt like an abandoned child and needed someone to help me out of my mysterious life."

The second day he was released by the police and was taken home by them. When they arrived home, Mary had just arrived too. He saw her crying and he remembered her saying to Tony "Go and get my son for me, I need him now."

When they entered, Mary was hitting Tony on the chest and when she turned around, she saw Peter. She held him in her arms and was crying, Peter was crying too. Joy was also crying and Ana joined them in the cry. They were unhappy with Tony's attitudes.

What had just happened had let Peter grow in knowledge and from then on he became like a stranger in Tony's house. He walked in fear, ate in fear and even slept in fear. Three weeks aftermath he was so sad to the extent that he couldn't control his emotions any longer. Peter was always crying and felt so bad about himself, finally, he ran away from home and began a new life in the street. Meanwhile, Mary was still in the city.

Life had not been so kind to me and I felt like an abandoned child wandering around the streets. I was determined not to ever return to Tony's home again. I thought life was meaningless and felt I wasn't meant for this world and I didn't care what might happen to me. I was so depressed. While walking and wandering about the streets, I immediately started to ask myself this question, "Is that what life is all about?" Where to stay wasn't my priority and what would happen to my education wasn't either. Afterwards, I went to a nearby town called Mushin, to see Lisa. Mushin is part of Lagos and was a busy place. The public transport available then was called MOLUE and DANFO. There are still much available today. Lisa lives in Mushin and was one of our family members too. I met Lisa

and her children and told her I'd be spending some days in her place. She was happy to see me, but so confused because she wasn't told I'd be visiting. That wasn't my problem, all I'd wanted was to stay away from Tony and Beki... By now, I had spent four days in Lisa's place. While still at Lisa's place, I managed to go to school.

One morning, after I arrived at school, one of my friends called Andrew informed me that Tony and Mary were looking for me. Hearing this, I quickly addressed a letter to Mary.

Dear Mother,

I am sorry for all that happened. I know you love me so much and I love you too. However, I'm not going back to Tony's home again. For the past four days I have been staying with Lisa and she will be sending his son to confirm my stay in her place. This is just to inform you. I will not be going to Lisa's place again because I know that Tony will soon be there to look for me. Mother don't worry God will look after me and I promise that I will be fine, I am sorry for everything.

Your son Peter.

It was a hard experience for Peter to write such a letter and he was contemplating if Andrew his friend should deliver the letter or not. Anyway, he gave the letter to him and instructed him to secretly give the letter to Mary. He knew they would come looking for him and he thought it would be wise to have plan B. After carefully considering the situation, he decided not to go to school again and ceased to go to Lisa's place too. He was still fourteen years old, Peter got no money to buy food or clothes to wear, the only cloth with him was the one he put in his school bag. After Andrew and Peter departed, he quickly changed from his school uniform to the clothes he had in his bag. Where to sleep that night was still a major concern to him, while looking around, he found a hidden place, an abandoned mini bus. He was so relieved because he knew the bus would soon be his place of refuge. He quickly put his school bag under the seat of the bus and went walking round the street to get acquainted with the place. He was hungry and got no money to buy food. He had to beg people for money. Unfortunately, no one gave him any. To survive became a problem. He went to the local garbage centre to look for bread that was thrown away by the bakery from the next street. The left over from the garbage centre had been his food for days.

Peter was getting tired and falling sick, his health condition was getting poorer and he needed money desperately to buy some medicine. He decided to go to the local market on the next day morning to look for a job. His objective was to carry loads for marketers, and people coming to buy goods. Sometimes he would put heavy loads on his head and sometimes he would use trolleys.

It was a hard job at his age but he enjoyed doing it. On his first day, Peter made some money which enabled him to buy medicine to take care of his health. He bought toothpaste, a brush and other essentials. The money he had made lasted for three days. Afterwards, he was sick again. He couldn't go to the market because of his poor health condition. Life living in the mini bus was another kind of experience for him. He lived-in the bus for several weeks. One day while he was still far asleep, someone opened the door of the bus. When he was about to run, the person got hold of him and said, "Don't panic," he was the owner of the abandoned bus where he used to sleep. He continued by saying, "I have been informed that someone was sleeping in my bus." Peter was afraid and didn't know what to do or say, the man said "I am here to confirm, who you are?" Before Peter could say a word, he threw another question to him, "why are you here?"

He was shaken and quickly said, "Sir I was here to pass the nights, I am sorry. Please let me go," said Peter. The man refused to let him go, Peter thought he was sent by Tony but his approach towards him was gentle. He said he wouldn't let him go. He asked, "Where are your parents?" His curiosity became high, he insisted to know the whereabouts of his parents. Peter was however convinced he wasn't sent by Tony and was sober and said,

"Sir, please let me go I don't have parents I've only got Mary," said Peter. He thought he would let him be but he didn't rather he said, "Okay then, take me to Mary." He thought he was dreaming when he told him to take him to Mary. Peter quickly said,

"Sir, please don't take me home, if you do, you are not doing me good, if you insist, I will go with you, but be warned, you will regret it if you take me home."

Peter was emotionally and completely sorry for himself. Sudden fear came over him and he was pathetic, shaking and shook for several minutes. After carefully noticing him, the man became merciful. He said, "Don't be afraid come with me and explain everything to me." Peter was relieved but was vigilant because he didn't know what would happen to him next. Although, he remembers the man's face, his face was familiar at the street. At least he was a little bit relieved after all.

The man lived five minutes away from where the mini bus was situated. After arriving at the man's home, Peter explained the entire predicament that happened to him. The man was moved with pity and kept saying, "I don't know what to do or what to say." He kept talking to himself for some time.

After a while he introduced himself, "My name is Robert, and you, what is your name?"

"My name is Peter." He told him to go to the bathroom and have a bath. He gave him clothes and food. Robert felt he should inform Peter's parents. He was scared not to get into trouble because of him, he needed Peter's opinion, and Peter could see how he was sympathetic with him. He was a kind person and was so kind to him. Peter felt he could talk to him freely, "Sir, you are right however this is what I want you to do for me. Mary is still in the city, you will go and see her. Tell Mary what has happened."

Peter knew she would be worried about him and perhaps his safety. He told Robert to tell her that he missed her but he would never go back to Tony's place again. He also insisted, "Tell her to do everything in her power to make sure that I do not return to Tony's house again. I know she would want to see me or try to know my whereabouts." As Robert was about to leave, Peter quickly rushed and said, "One more thing Robert, tell her I will arrange for her to see me, tell Joy I miss her too," said Peter.

Before he left to Tony's place, where to stay was still an issue. Robert had previously told Peter that he can't stay in his place. His wife and kids were on holiday and they would soon be back. Peter's situation was problematic for him and he wanted to find a solution for him, in fact, he was confused. Peter could remember saying to him, "Don't worry Sir; I will look after myself before they arrive and perhaps, I will get another place. Please sir."

"Okay," replied Robert.

Chapter 7: Meeting with Mary

Robert had just arrived from Tony's place where he went to see Mary. The smile in his face was tremendous and I knew he would have something good to tell me when he returned. Without hesitation, he commenced to explain the outcome of his visit.

He then suddenly shouted, "PETER I'M BACK." He saw Mary. She was so happy to hear that I was well. I was excited and wanted to hear more, I quickly asked him, "What happened next, and how did it go?" My worries were, I was troubled because I wasn't sure if they'd come looking for me. Robert noticed me and said,

"No Peter I didn't give them my home address. I couldn't have done something like that, after knowing all you'd gone through?" He told me, Mary insisted and he gave her one of his friends address. His friend lived in the next street. After hearing what he'd said, I was relieved and I asked him a further question, "I hope Mary and Joy are okay?" I was curious and just wanted to know more. Robert and I went inside the lounge and he narrated everything to me in details.

He saw a woman with Mary. He thought she might be Beki. He had to excuse Mary from her so that they could have their conversation in private. Robert described the woman he saw, she was tall and was fair in complexion. The woman he saw was Beki. I was glad that he excused Mary from her. Robert continued narrating the outcome of his visit. Mary was comfortable with his visit and was happy if I could stay away from Tony and Beki. All she'd wanted is for me to have peace elsewhere. She was worried about my education. She insisted to see me, perhaps, somewhere tonight. Hearing that, I was scared and thought what of, if something went wrong again? I'd like to see her too but I wouldn't like anything funny to happen to me again. After having thought about it, I concluded, not to see her soon and thought it was too early to do so. What of, if something went wrong?

Robert persuaded me and wanted me to reason with him why I must see Mary that night,

"Listen Peter she is your mum," said Robert. The funniest thing was that he'd already arranged with her to meet me in his friend's place that same night at 8:00pm.

We then laid a plan on how to meet Mary. In fact, I didn't know what to believe, everything was sudden, was it a plan for Robert to hand me over to Tony? But, why would he do that? I thought it would be impossible for him to betray me. He was a kind man. Nevertheless, I told Robert how I wanted it to be done. I said to him, "You go alone to your friend's house and I'll join you later." I'll be around somewhere before Mary arrives. I want to be sure she is alone and that, she isn't followed. After telling Robert what the plan was, I wanted his opinion too. I then asked "What do you think to that?"

"Okay Peter that is a brilliant idea, I won't like anything else to happen to you, after all you went through," replied Robert. I thanked Robert and appreciated his help in this matter. My situation was hard for me to bear alone and I'd appreciated Robert's support.

"It's okay Peter; I hope all will be well soon," said Robert.

In the evening of that day, the night fell so quickly. It was around 7:00pm. I made my way towards the nearest hideout. It was close to Robert's friend's house. My location where I was hiding was clear of any obstructions and my position enabled me to see every movement.

At around 7:30pm, I saw Mary coming in a distance. I kept a close eye on her, she was alone and look depressed in the way she walked. After a few minutes, she made her way to the main entrance of Robert's friend house. About ten minutes later, Robert made his way to the same place. I waited for a few minutes before I decided to join them at the same place but I wasn't comfortable with the whole arrangement and I thought it would be in my best interest to slightly change the plan and decided not to join them soon. I sent a friend who I'd just met to speak to Robert and inform him about my plan. While my new friend was on his way to bring them to my hideout which was not far away from Robert's friend's place. While they were on the way, I kept a close eye on them. I was satisfied that they were not being followed by Tony or anyone else. Robert wasn't happy with the new plan but reasoned with me and later supported me. He realised that I had already made up my mind and wouldn't take any chances, not after all that I had went through. As soon as my new friend left, I quickly changed my location to a closer one. After a while, I saw Mary and Robert exiting the building and were making their way towards my hiding place. They were looking for me and didn't realise that I had changed my location. After carefully watching their movements, I appeared to them from an unpredicted hideout. My meeting with Mary was well planned. Mary had been looking forward to seeing me too, as soon as she got sight of me, it was too emotional for her. The feeling was tremendous. I then called her, "Mother." I hugged her she hugged me too and started crying as she always does. She said to me, "My son, but, why you are so in pain?" The way and the manner she said it was pathetic and her words came to me as a question and the thought never left me, "Was it true I was in pain?" The emotion was too much that Robert was moved to tears too. I was happy to see Mary. In fact, it was one of our best moments but we were uncomfortable because, she didn't want Tony to see us. I was afraid too and it was a worrying moment for me. Robert noticed that we weren't comfortable talking, he however took us to a nearest restaurant. The restaurant was one of the best in the area at that time and people around Ilogbo, Olokodana, Oto and Oyingbo in Lagos like coming to have a nice time there. In fact, that was the first time I have been to such a place. We ate some food and had a discussion at length. Mary said she would speak to Albert and Ana and would let them to reason with her. She advised Robert to come to the house too. She intended to have a meeting with Tony, Albert and Ana Albert's wife. Mary wanted Robert to attend the meeting as well and would emphasise that they leave me alone and let me be. She added, "Peter, I will strongly stand by you and I won't give up, even if it would cause me my life." Her words gave me courage. She insisted, Tony must let me be.

Robert didn't argue with her either, he thought the idea wasn't bad. "I will come to the house but won't disclose that Peter is in my place," said Robert. After saying that, he asked my opinion on the matter. I was confused and didn't know what to say, "It's okay," said Peter.

The deal was made and we would be departing shortly. Before leaving, Mary said, she needed a week to get the meeting arranged. Soon afterwards, we separated. It was a happy moment for Mary, Robert and I. We were relieved however, were eager and worried what the outcome of the next meeting would be.

Nevertheless, I was so happy for our meeting. I was always suspicious of what might happen to me next. I was hoping that the future would be good and I put my faith in what the future would have for me. The worst things I would not have wished

to happen to me at that time, was to live with Tony again.

Robert and I went home. At least for the first time in my life, I had lots of jokes and fun with Robert. A question kept coming to my mind. Will that be the beginning or the end of my predicament? What do you think?

Chapter 8: At Tony's Place

One evening, before the end of that same week, Mary invited Robert to Tony's place. It was astonishing that, things started happening quickly after Mary last visited us. However, Robert had been looking forward to it too and soon he would start preparing to leave for Tony's place. For obvious reasons, I decided to move away temporarily from Robert's place. I wasn't sure what might happen after his return, so I decided to leave for the time being, until the air was clear.

It was over three hours that Robert left for Tony's place I was worried why he hadn't returned. Two hours later Robert arrived. It was not so easy to guess whether he brought good news or not, he was such a lively person and it wasn't easy to know when he was serious or not. In fact he was a jovial person. In his usual style, he commenced to explain the outcome of his visit, "Hi Peter." After greeting me, he told me he met someone on the way while still on the way to Tony's place and was directed to Albert's my uncle's house. He met Ana Albert's wife. After a few minutes, Albert came in too. He greeted him, after a brief introduction, Albert said, "Mary, Peter's mum has already explained all that took place to me." It was interesting for Robert to notice that Albert who cut me with a blade and flogged me repeatedly was now interested in my affairs. I was surprised to hear Robert say that Albert gave an instruction and planned his next meeting with Tony.

He said, imitating Albert's voice, "WHAT SHALL WE DO NOW?" The question came as a surprise to Robert and he said, "I don't know." Robert told Albert to tell him what he had in mind. I was anxious and lacking patience, I just wanted him to tell me the whole thing that happened. Since he is a jovial person, he wouldn't stop to make me laugh at the same time, "Not again Robert," he started imitating Albert's voice again.

"BOTH OF US WILL BE VISITING TONY SHORTLY. WHEN WE GET TO TONY'S PLACE, YOU HAVE TO PRETEND YOU HAVE NEVER MET MARY BEFORE," According to their plan, Albert will say that someone directed Robert to him and even outline what he must say to capture Tony's attention. This is what you have to say to all of us, "Peter approached you on the street, he gave you Albert's address. He said he is very sorry for all that had happened and he wanted Albert to plead on his behalf." That wasn't a problem with Robert, after all, all he wanted was for me to have the peace of mind. After carefully listening to what Albert had said, he replied, "its okay by me."

A few minutes later, Albert and Robert made their way to Tony's place, when they got there they saw Tony, Mary and Beki. Robert did according to the plan and Mary pretended she hadn't or never met him before. After explaining things to Tony as planned, suddenly he flew up with anger saying, "Where is the stupid boy, where is he? BRING HIM HERE NOW!" Tony was furious, noticing his actions, Albert replied, "Take it easy Tony, if you continue this way this boy will runaway again."
Albert thought they should be thankful that I was found again. Hearing what Albert had just said, Tony started screaming, "No I don't care and I don't want to see him again."
There was tension between them all and Tony wouldn't yield either. Mary was crying and was speechless. Robert was disappointed with Tony's attitude. After a while Albert told Robert to leave. Before he departed Albert promised to talk to Tony at the later time, hopefully he would listen to him. Mary was still crying when Robert left and everyone was disappointed at Tony's behaviour. This was how Robert narrated the outcome of his visit.
I was thankful to him. He was just a caring person. He had supported me during my hard times and had become not only a friend but a brother. With the look of things, it appeared that Tony didn't want to care about me any longer. Even if he did, I didn't either want

to stay with him again. I was comfortable staying with Robert and I also thought it would be wise to give myself a sense of freedom but as a child, all of these were too hard for me to understand or bear. From that time on, I started to think of what to do to help myself. I felt like an abandoned child or someone that had no future.

Not too long, I was told by a friend who I'd just met a few weeks before that there would be a city marathon race. I then decided to enrol in the race. A month later, I was among the candidates that took part in the race. I completed about 42.195km. Unfortunately, I didn't make it to the first position. My position was amongst the first 20s and I was given two tin-can of chocolate powder and t-shirts for completing the race. That was the first Milo Marathon race that took place in Surulere Stadium Lagos Nigeria.

There were thousands of people who participated in the race. I remembered that I aimed to win a prize, the feelings I got for education was high and I had always wanted to go to school. I watched my contemporaries going to schools but I'd always stayed at home or moving around the streets without doing anything. My ambition then was to take part in the race. Maybe, I would win a prize to sponsor my education. Unfortunately, I regretted I didn't make it. However, the race gave me courage, determination, zeal and endurance. I was so determined that my aspirations were so high and my dreams had become a reality to me. I knew that my hardship, my suffering would end one day. I was hoping for this day and it had become my everyday dreams.

I was still living in Robert's place when his wife and children were back from holiday. This was a worrying situation for him as predicted. Robert's family and I stayed together for at least two weeks, after the end of the two weeks, he arranged that I stay with his aunt Lola, she lived in the same street as him and Lola had five children. Three boys with two girls, one of her children was living abroad while three were going to school locally and one was in university. Lola stayed in a five bed room flat which was big and there were lots of spaces around it. I was told to share a room with her other three children. The room had got five beds in it. There was one

single bed, with two bunk beds. I was given one of the bunk beds. That had been my sleeping bed for at least some period. Robert explained the difficulties I had been going through to Lola. She was so sad after hearing all that I have gone through and was moved with pity. She promised to help me back to school and to let me continue education abroad in the later period. Her comments came to me as a surprise and it was like a dream that good things were starting to come my way. I was already looking forward to it. Having this dream in mind, I was happy and was grateful for Robert's help. For me, this was too good to be true "My God, I will be living in Lola's house."

By now, I was fifteen years old and I was still staying in Lola's place. Mary had moved to the village and she was happy that I was saved with Robert. Sometimes, I did visit her in the village but, she was always worried about my education.

Lola lived a double life and would change boyfriends every month. I thought she would treat me as she had promised, unfortunately for me I was treated as a servant of the house.

I cooked meals and washed clothes every day until late in the night, I slept late every night and it was hard for me to get at least three hours sleep per night. She woke me up every 4:00am and no days were exceptional. Sometimes she would slap me for minor mistakes. Her boyfriends and some of her children also treated me the same way too. I knew Robert won't be happy to hear of what I was going through at the hand of Lola and her children. I was scared to tell Robert; I didn't want to create a problem between both of them. One day, I approached Lola to discuss about my education, but beforehand it was difficult for me to do so. I was always scared to talk or ask her questions but however picked up the courage on that day, "Good afternoon Lola"

"Good afternoon Peter, how are you?" I was shaken and rambled in words and quickly replied, "I am fine ma." Afterwards, I asked her a question, "Ma, any idea when I will be enrolling to school?" Before I could asked another question, she slapped me repeatedly. She kicked me and quickly ran into the room, picked my clothes and started throwing them away through the window at the stairways. It was terrible to see her in such a mood. I was confused and regretted that I asked her such a question. As I was trying to beg, she shouted at me, "Get out of my home, you are just a slave, you thought I would waste my money on your education? Go away, I never want to set my eyes on you again" said Lola.

I fell on my feet begging for mercy, "Please I am sorry, forgive me don't throw me outside, I have no place to go." She was firm with her decision and wouldn't listen to my cry. One of her boyfriends was also around at the time. He said to her,

"MAKE SURE YOU SEND THAT BOY AWAY." A few minutes after her boyfriend's comments, I was thrown outside. I thought life wasn't treating me well and I was so sorry for myself. I kept asking these questions to myself "What a life? Or when will all these dreadful things end?" I didn't know what to do, say or who to turn to. I was confused about my predicament. Aftermath, I was reluctant but however I started picking up my belongings that were thrown away by Lola. Soon afterwards, as I was about to leave the compound, one of Lola's daughters had just arrived from the school. Seeing me in such a state of mind, she was moved with pity. After hearing what her mother had just did to me. She quickly rushed to Lola's room and confronted her. I was afraid to stay behind. I gently exited the main entrance gate and made my way to the street again.

While still walking on the street, I saw Robert and Lola's daughter Florence running towards me. Florence quickly grasped my bag in a haste and quickly said,

"You have to stay with us, please don't go, my mother's attitude was evil. Please come back with us." Hearing what she had just said, Robert replied,

"No he is not going back there, my aunt's character is bad, I had told her several times to keep her promise towards Peter but she wouldn't listen." At this stage, it was obvious that Robert had lost confidence in Lola's character. In a soft voice he told me, "Listen Peter, returning to Lola's place would be detrimental for you and perhaps a waste of time." He didn't want me to live with Lola again and thought I had enough trouble in my entire life. He suggested to take me to his friend's house but however wanted to think about it. I was persuaded by him and was instantly taken to his place. Later that evening, I was taken to Robert's friend's house. His name was Emanuel. He lived and worked locally as a driver in a hotel which was about three miles away from his home and his street where he lives, was a bit further from his home. After getting off his street, you have to walk through a tiny narrow way for at least about two minutes before you get to his place. He was a bachelor but had a girlfriend. Robert agreed with him that I pass the night at his home. The arrangement was for a temporary period. I was grateful to Robert and his friend Emanuel. Florence, Lola's daughter was with us too. After the arrangement has been made, Robert and Florence left. I was thankful to them. In fact they stood by me. To me, it was just like a start of a new journey which I wasn't sure of my destination but I was hopeful and assumed that all would be over soon. I was demoralised, weakened and lacked self-esteem. I wished vile things for myself and felt rejected. I was lonely and that wasn't a big deal for me anyway, since I have been used to it.

It had been weeks now, and not so long, Mary visited Robert's place. She was directed to see me at Emanuel's place and had been told of everything that took place at Lola's place. Although, she had previously warned me against staying in Lola's place. Soon afterwards, she came to see me. Emanuel's room was small and with a double bed in it. Mary was uncomfortable to stay for a longer period of time. It was good to see her again and her presence was a fortification to me. I remembered all that she said to me before she left. Holding my two hands, she stared into my eyes and said, "My son, I am going back to the village. Tony has become poorer and his condition is not improving either." I was anxious and wanted to know more but she was breaking in speech and crying at the same time.

Crying wasn't a new phenomenon to me, as she always cried for my sake. She wasn't happy to see me in that condition; all she had wished was for me to return to a full time education. She promised to raise money to help support my education. I was so delighted with her comments and said, "Mum, I understand. You have tried for me, please go back to the village. I will also try and look for a job may be, I will raise some money too." After hearing what I had just said. She decided to leave but however, she would be going back to the village on the following day. She also told me that, Albert and his other relations had visited Tony. They warned him to handle me with care. It was difficult for her to leave, after saying goodbye, she suddenly started a new conversation. She said, "My son, with the look of things, I assume Tony is now regretting." I was now getting fed up to talk about Tony and wanted to change the topic. I quickly said,

"Okay mum, please can we leave Tony out of this?" I thought that, that was the end.

"One more thing" She said, "One of your uncles in the village, the one who looks after things while I was at the city had just died two days ago. The burial ceremony is next week. Tony, Joy and Albert's family will be attending. Please do me a favour and come too," said Mary.

"Mum, I am fed up of Tony and would not like to see him at the moment, I don't think this would be a good idea," I replied. She liked persuading me for such things, "Listen Peter, you are not coming to see Tony. You are coming to visit me. Remember it was a long time we had stayed together as a family. Don't you know that I miss you?" I was touched with her comment and I thought I missed her too. Without hesitation, I said, "I miss you too mum." Afterwards, I promised to be at the burial ceremony. After a while she left and we then separated. It was good to see her again and I would be looking forward to see her soon perhaps in the village.

Chapter 9: THE UNEXPECTED TRUTH

August 1985. The month and the year, this period has been an unforgettable memory. Five days after Mary left, I travelled to the village as promised. For me, I just wanted to be there perhaps to see her and to be close to her, not for the burial ceremony. When I arrived at the village, I saw lots of people partying. Everywhere was crowded with people. I decided to take the back way. I wanted Mary to see me and be aware that I was around however, I didn't intend to stay long in the village, and I tried to avoid Tony as much as I could. Beki was at the ceremony too and there were lots of family members. Joy was happy to see me. I had to keep my distance from her because she was always with Tony. Joy knew I was around, but Tony, Beki and others including Mary had not gained sight of me yet. While moving and trying to find out where Mary was, it happened just like a day dream. As I was about to continue through a sharp corner, someone shouted, "HEY YOU, COME HERE." I was wondering who that was. The person continued saying, "DON'T YOU NO HOW TO GREET?" This person happened to be a strange woman which I had never met before. Politely, I said to her,

"Ma I had just greeted before," I greeted her again, "Good afternoon." She just shouted at me, "OKAY WHATEVER." As I was about going my way, she shouted again asking me a question, "WHO ARE YOUR PARENTS IN THIS VILLAGE?" I was reluctant to reply. However I told her that my parents were Mary and Tony.

I thought that would be the end of it, but it wasn't. She asked again, "Did you just say Tony?" Before I could say YES, she threw another question at me, "Which of the Tony," before I could reply to that one too, she asked me another question, "Was it the one staying in the city?" I was getting bored with the conversation and I wanted to see Mary as soon as possible. I quickly and in a rush replied,

"YES MA." The woman wouldn't give up asking me questions, after a while she asked,

"What is your own name?"

"My name is Peter," said I. She repeated the name again three times.

"Peter, Peter and Peter," looking straight into my eyes, she asked, "Did you just say Peter?"

"Yes, I'm Peter." Immediately I said yes, she started crying. She cried and confessed saying, "Death. Death you have done so many bad things. Is it not this same boy that was brought to the village as a baby? My God, you have grown big." In the first instance, I wondered what she was talking about however, her words rang a bell. I then asked her in a low tone of voice," What did you just say?" I wanted to be sure of what I heard and I wanted her to repeat the same. The look in her eye showed that perhaps she was sorry for me but I wondered why, after all, she was drunk. Suddenly she said,

"Your mother died long ago and your father left you in the village." Hearing that, I was mad with myself and quickly said, "No that isn't true, my mother is Mary. Please tell me it's not true. You must be joking. Aren't you?" As the conversation became intense, a passer-by who happened to know the woman interrupted our conversation. He said to her, "You drunkard, leave the boy alone." I thought it was a joke or perhaps what she said was because she was under the influence of alcohol. I was in a haste and rushed to see Mary. I was shaking, when I found her, I felt she had been lying to me. It was tense in the conversation and in a hasty voice I lamented, "Who are you mother? Are you my real mother? Tell me the truth about your self or lie to me and I will disown you forever. Who are you mother?" Hearing what I had just said, she knew that something was wrong somewhere.

She fell on her feet crying and saying, "Help me God, could somebody help me, please help me." her mood was pathetic, she couldn't talk. She was crying heavily. A standby woman, who knew Tony quickly called his attention. When Tony came in, Mary grieved accusing him, "This is it, and you caused it all," said Mary. I was angry and started believing that something was definitely wrong somewhere. I explained to Tony that I was told Mary wasn't my mother that my biological mother died and you left me in the village. Looking straight into his eyes, I added, "I need an explanation dad."

As Tony was about to change the conversation, Mary swift in with anger and said, "ENOUGH IS ENOUGH Tell him I'm not his biological mother, tell him the truth." You needed to see the look in her face, in fact Mary was devastated. I didn't even care, all I had wanted was to know the truth and the circumstances surrounding my birth. After just a few seconds, with anger I asked, "Mother, say it isn't true. Tell me you are my mother or aren't you?" I was crying and was so sad it was like my day was turning to a nightmare and thought I was dreaming. Seeing me in a bad mood, Mary was moved with pity and I was told the story of my life. This was how it all started. It was late in the evening, the day was so bright and from the glance of the window, I could see the birds flying and singing in the sky. It was so beautiful but my heart was full of pain. Suddenly, I was told that my mother died when I was seven months old. Joy was about three years old and Vincent was five. Few years later Tony, Mary and the entire family decided to keep the truth away from me and I was not knowledgeable of who my real mother was.

I was told that Vincent and Joy were later aware of the situation but had been warned not to disclose the truth of the matter to me. I was also told that Mary and Tony were blood brother and sister. Albert whom I have known as my uncle was cousin to Tony and Mary. All these were terrible news to my hearing and I was deeply upset. I didn't know what to do or say, I was short of words. Tony told me it was the idea of Mary that he got married and she insisted that we needed a stepmother. Tony loved my biological mother dearly and decided not to remarry again but he couldn't resist the temptation not to marry Beki. In fact, I was told so many things. It was on the same evening that I was told Mary had no child of her own and that I was the only son she had looked after but I was not legally adopted. This was a family arrangement. Tai and Janet whom I thought were my blood sisters were daughters of Tony and Mary's other cousins. I was finally told that my biological mother was Elizabeth. My blood brother and sister were Vincent and Joy. I was also told Elizabeth has got blood brothers and sisters. Immediately the truth became apparent, I became angry and kept saying… "But why, why could you have kept the truth away for so long?" Mary was still crying and was upset too. The situation was embarrassing. She wasn't comfortable neither was I. However, I quickly hugged her saying, "Mum I don't care, all I know is that, you are my mother. So don't worry about all that took place."

She was still crying and was speechless. The room was silent for several minutes, everybody was moved with pity, and it was so emotional. This is the first time I saw Beki crying too. It was the first time I saw her crying for my sake. It was so funny to see Tony crying. He cried like a baby. Mary was later accompanied by a friend for counselling. I was traumatised as the result of what had just happened but who really cared about me? It was a shocking experience of my life to have discovered that Mary was not my biological mother. Anyway, I took heart and decided to move on with my traumatic experience. It was now late in the night. The burial ceremony continued until late in the night. When the burial ceremony was over, everybody left for the city. I decided to stay with Mary at the village for two weeks. My attitude remained the same and we tried to console each other. Mary explained lots of things to me. I left the village but promised to see her as soon as I can. Before leaving the village, we both held hands. I said to her, "Mum, no mater what has happened, you remain the same in my heart. You are my mother that I knew. I love you mum." She was so pleased to hear me say that. As soon as I stepped outside, many questions started floating in my mind. I started talking to myself, what was going to happen aftermath? Was the event that took place going to affect Mary and me? Since the cat has been left out of the bag, what to do next? Leaving Mary's place, I didn't know where to go and I was confused about my movement or who to turn to for advice. I asked myself again, Will I return to Tony's place in the city again? I was thinking about my future too and was so curious to discover what the future held for me. I thought this might just be the beginning of a tougher challenge. But for how long would I continue like this? Something rang a bell to my hearing, what could that have been?

Chapter 10: The New House Boy

As soon as Peter was back to the city, he went to see Robert his friend. He explained everything that had taken place at the village. Robert was shocked to hear him speak about his ordeal, his advice and understanding fortified him at least for the night. They stayed together till late in the evening. Later that evening, Peter returned to Emanuel's place.

Two days later he started looking for a job so that he could help Emanuel by contributing towards payment of the rent. It was very hard to find a job at his age. Few weeks after his return from the village, it was hard and food was the only thing he needed to survive with. He was being fed by neighbours and friends. Florence Lola's daughter was also amongst those who fed him. He could remember, she used to throw bread, tomato, onions and tin of sardines through Lola's first floor kitchen window. Before she threw any of this food, she would give him a signal with her finger. Afterwards she would throw the foods. The food was usually thrown one after another. Peter was so grateful to her. At least he could have food in his belly.

One day, Emanuel came back from work. He said, "Peter, I have found you a job." But he wasn't sure if he would be pleased with the kind of job he found. He was hesitating to talk. Peter was eager too and wanted him to break the news as soon as he could. He was running out of patience and quickly said, "Listen, I will do anything. Tell me please, I can't wait."

"Okay, my director is looking for someone to look after his father," said Emanuel.

"Look after his father?" Peter asked.

"Yes, his father, he is eighty-five years old and the wages are poor. The good thing is that, you will be living in the man's place," said Emanuel. Peter was surprised when he said he would be staying with his director's father and wanted to know more about the job,

"Staying in his place? Does that mean that, I will be working as a houseboy, and how long have you known this fellow?" Peter asked.

"Yes, it is houseboy," replied Emanuel. He didn't know the man too well but was told he was a character and had thrown out four houseboys out of his home. Lots of people have refused to work for him and Emanuel was wondering if that would be the right place for Peter. He was not too sure and after given brief thought about it, Peter jumped into conclusion,

"I will do it, don't worry I'm going to cope. After all, who cares about me?" Emanuel was unhappy with Peter's comment. He said quickly, "No, I think you can't. I was told that the man was inhuman beside the wages are too low." It wasn't a problem for Peter, all he had wished for was to work and feed himself, "Okay, let me just give it a try," he replied. Peter wasn't sure about his decision and he was thinking if he had made the right choice but thought he needed to do something to sustain himself.

Two days later. Joy and Robert came to visit him at Emanuel's place. She was desperate to talk to Peter. Her body language told him that she had important information for him. Immediately she saw him, she said, "Tony is looking for a way to make you come back home. He is planning to visit Mary for a discussion. I have come to warn you. Please stay away from him." Peter was fearful because he didn't want to live with Tony either, noticing that, she held his hands and said, "Think about it, I don't want you to go through those pains again." Robert was kind too. He brought him some money and bread. He said, "Listen to your sister." He was such a generous man and his generosity has been part of him, he indeed stood by Peter. At least Peter was glad that their visits strengthened him. He was contemplating he should tell them about the houseboy job but thought Joy might discourage him to do it. Finally, both of them left. Peter stayed behind because he didn't want anyone to take sight of him or know where he lived.

A week later, Emanuel took him to see his director for an interview. His director's name was Mosu, he was a gentle man. After finishing interviewing him, he was still not convinced if he could work with his father. Peter remembered lying to him about his age, that wasn't a problem anyway since he didn't require any paperwork for his interview. He was later taken to Mr. Benson's house. Meanwhile, he had just been separated and seized to stay with Emanuel. Mr. Benson's home would soon be his dwelling place. Peter thanked Emanuel for his help and hospitality during his stay at his place.

He was taken with a white van to Mr Benson's place at Idi-Oro Mushin in Lagos. He lived in a semi-detached house which was about ten kilometres away from where Emanuel lived. Mr. Benson's son Mosu drove behind them. They drove for about half an hour. When they arrived and as Peter was about to greet Mr. Benson, he shouted, "IS THAT MY NEW HOUSE BOY?"

His son replied, "Dad, don't start again. Don't mess around with this new boy. If you do, I will not look for another person to look after you," said Mosu. Before they could make their way towards his living room, he shouted again,

"COME HERE, YOU IDIOT." Mosu was angry to hear his dad calling Peter idiot, "Stop dad, and behave yourself. Stop frightening the poor boy." Mosu advised Peter to ignore his dad. He said Peter will soon get used to him. Before Mosu could finish talking to Peter, Mr. Benson pushed him out of the way and shouted again,

"GET OUT OF MY WAY, YOU IDIOT."

"Stop it dad, his name is not idiot. Call him Peter," said Mosu. As Peter was about to tell Mosu that he can't stay with his dad, he was nervous and frightened. Peter kept his silence and he was imagining whether to go back to Emanuel's place or not, nevertheless, he kept thinking. He thought, it was a challenge, but could he cope with Mr. Benson's problems? Anyway, he decided to give it a try, at least his son was a nice man, maybe with time he would get used to him. After staying for a while, Mosu left and promised to see them in a couple of weeks' time. Mr. Benson was a tall man and was about 6ft tall. Instantaneously as his son left he shouted, "Hey Idiot." Anyway,

Peter had been advised by Mosu to ignore him anytime he called him idiot. Peter's first night at his place was terrible. After finishing

cleaning the home and doing other tasks he was assigned to do, he went to bed at around 11:00pm and at 1:00am while he was fast asleep, he suddenly heard someone shouting, he thought the noise which he heard was from outside or next-door but it wasn't. He later realised that it was Mr. Benson. He listened carefully to be certain that it was him. After certainly convinced that it was him, he however walked towards his bedroom. While on about two metre away distance from him, he asked,

"Sir, I hope all is well?" He didn't reply to his question. Mr. Benson looked alright. Peter asked him the second time, "Sir, I hope all is well?" Still no reply, as he advanced a step towards him, Peter sat close to him. He kept shouting at least, in every ten to fifteen minutes. He was scared, his actions frightened him. At about 3:00am Peter called his son Mosu on the phone and explained all that took place. He was shocked with his reply when he said,

"My dad is okay, he is deliberately doing that to scare you. Go to bed boy."

Peter couldn't say a word, "Okay sir." Peter's fright became intensive and he was wondering

Why would he try to scare him off?

A few minutes later he returned to his room. He didn't find it funny. Mr. Benson kept shouting until 5:00am in the morning. Peter was sleepless at night but he managed to sleep at least for one hour, when Peter woke up around 6:00am, he immediately commenced his domestic tasks. The second night wasn't different from the previous night. The third night was the worst I had ever experienced with him. On that very night, he would be singing and sometime stood off his bed and would walk in and out the corridors. He also clapped his hands and would be shouting at the same time. The forth night was manageable in comparable with the first and second nights. At the daybreak of the forth night, Mr. Benson called him names and would sometimes swear and uses abusive speeches on him. Peter was so worried and concerned about his safety. He was counting on the day Mosu would arrive. Two weeks later, Mosu visited them as was promised. Without hesitation, Peter said, "Sir I am sorry that I have to leave. You are a kind man, unfortunately, I have to leave. I am very sorry. Please forgive me." Peter thought he would be angry with him. He was surprised with his comment when he said, "I understand and aware that my father is hard to cope with. I just wanted to give it a try however, you are a nice boy too, don't worry, I know that it would be difficult for you to cope with him," said Mosu. He gave Peter some money and wished him well. When he was about to leave, he thanked him and wished him well too. There is one more thing. As he said goodbye to Mr. Benson, he was amused with his response when he shouted, "GOODBYE," Soon afterwards, I left them for good.

Chapter 11: My New Job

Life after leaving Mr. Benson's place, Peter didn't know where he would be heading to. While still on the way, he started thinking of what to do. He thought it might be good to return to Emanuel's place but, thought it wouldn't be a good idea to do so. Robert and Emanuel have tried and had done lots for his sake. It wasn't a good idea either to see Robert at this stage. Peter however went to a nearby restaurant. He was hungry and needed food before he continued with his journey. It was getting too late. The night had fallen so quick and he was still on the street wandering about. He started imagining on what his next step would be. Suddenly, he started talking to himself again. He thought he was being insane but how can he be insane and still know about it. Passers-by, who happen, going by foot, would shake their heads and pass by him. The trauma he was experiencing was too much to bear and the last thing he wanted to do was to return to Tony's place again. As he was considering doing that, he remembered Joy had warned him not to do so. How can he think of such things, not after all he had gone through at his hands, "Hmm" Peter was completely stressed and worried, it was dark and he couldn't even figure out what the time was. He was afraid, panicked and was unable to control his emotions. Suddenly, he started crying. As he moved a little bit further, he saw an uncompleted building and thought it would be a good idea for him to pass the night there. He went into the uncompleted building and passed the night. The next day, he decided to see Robert and Emanuel in order to explain all that had taken place. He didn't have anywhere else to go to. They had been good friends to him. That very morning, Peter was moody and there were tears falling out of his eyes. He wasn't crying but he couldn't explain why tears were fluctuating.

While waiting at the next bus stop a man approached him and said, "For some time now, I have been watching you. Why are you crying?" He asked. His question wasn't a surprise to him, however,

He added, "I hope all is well with you?" Peter was reluctant to answer him. The more he tried to answer the questions, the intensive his tears were. The man was moved with pity and started persuading Peter to talk. He asked, "What is it? If there is any problem, tell me, and stop crying," said the man. He sounded consolable and Peter thought he was talking to himself when he said, "Sir I need a job" Not realising he was actually giving an answer to the man's question. Hearing that, the man said, "Job"

He again asked, "How old are you?"

"I am fifteen years old," Peter quickly said.

"Fifteen years, looking for a full time job?" As Peter was about to speak, he asked again, "But why are you not in school?" Peter didn't want to reply and was so sorry when he said, "sir it's a long story" instantaneously, he introduced himself,

"My name is Lemmy Isa, call me Lemmy." Lemmy was security personnel in a security guard company. He was an influential man in the firm where he worked, after having a conversation with Peter at length, Lemmy promised to give him a job so that he would be able to feed himself. Peter was however surprised and got scared when he insisted to see his parents. As he tried to persuade him, Peter explains all that he went through and insisted he couldn't see his parents. Although, he told him about Robert, Lemmy requested to see him. Peter thought they were to meet Robert another time. However, they both entered a bus at the next bus stop to see Robert. He was still wondering of what might happen next. Arriving at Robert's place, he was surprised with our visit but delighted to see Lemmy and Peter. Without hesitation, Robert wanted to know what brought us to his place. He asked "Why are you here Peter?" After explaining all Peter had gone through at the hands of Mr. Benson, Robert introduced himself to Lemmy and explained lots of things that had happened. Lemmy was shocked and shook his head. He said, "Listen Peter, your situation is a touching one I am sorry that you went through all this," said Lemmy. Peter was so happy to hear him saying "I think I will help you get a security guard job" His comment came to him as the biggest news he had wanted. He was grateful to him and said, "I appreciate the help sir"

Robert was happy too, Lemmy gave Peter his office address and asked him to see him first thing the next day morning. Before departing, Peter begged Robert to allow him pass the night at his place.

The next day, Peter went to Lemmy's office. Arriving at his office, he saw a long queue. It was difficult to get into the main office entrance. After waiting in queue for about an hour he saw a woman coming out from the building, he told her that he was here to see Lemmy, "Lemmy Isa" the woman asked his name and went in to call Lemmy. After a while, he came and took him out of the queue. Peter was given an application form to complete, which he did. The position available was day security guard position but he had wanted and preferred night guard position and quickly said "I prefer night" Lemmy wasn't happy with his response.

He said, "Peter, the only position available is day position," he replied. Peter knew it would be unkind on his part to decide on what position and shift he chooses, to avoid further conversation, he said "Okay sir and thanks for the offer."

Lemmy was a kind man too. Peter would have preferred night. He knew night could have been good for him and he would at least be somewhere safe at night. The day was alright too but where would he pass the night? Peter had no home either, or have a place to sleep at night. He couldn't stay at Robert's place or either stay in Emanuel's place. His girlfriend felt his presence disturbs their freedom. Peter had no choice than to accept the day security offer. He was posted to an international shipping company. The company deals with cocoa and cashew nuts by shipping them abroad. The company was owned by Elder Dempster Agency known as EDA. Peter was posted to Company A and was given a security guard uniform. His shift was to start on the next day. He quickly rushed to Robert's place to pick few of his clothes and left his big bag behind. His only problem at that time was where to pass the night. He thought he was bothering Robert and Emanuel and perhaps he was inconveniencing their privacy. Nevertheless, they were not complaining, the night fell so soon and Peter decided to return to the uncompleted building where he had once passed the night. Apart from that, he was happy for his new job and he vowed to give his first salary to Mary. To him, it was a journey of life and a new beginning. Peter was looking forward to start work at 8:00 am on the next day. However, he arrived early to get acquainted with the place. He was there an hour before and met the security supervisor named Sylvester at Company A, after introducing himself, he took him to show him the surroundings of the site. Peter entered the toilet re-freshened himself and also brushed his teeth. He then afterwards put on his new security uniform. He was smart in the uniform and was later introduced to Jack, Lawrence, Noah and Helen. The day was busy and there were trailers, Lorries and buses coming in and out of the building. His shift ended at 6:00pm in the evening. He was satisfied and colleagues were pleased with his first performance. At least he would be making new friends. His colleagues treated him with care they thought he was too young for the position. After leaving for the day, Peter felt he needed to treat himself. He still got some money remaining and however went to a local restaurant to eat. In fact he did enjoy the meal. The night had fallen and he had nowhere to sleep rather than the uncompleted building. The uncompleted building was his home for over one month and the work place toilet had been his bathroom where he normally took his shower.

Night at the uncompleted building had been terrible and unforgettable for him. His room mates were rats, lizards, mosquitoes, frogs and flies. It was very hard for him to sleep at that environment. He was always awake at the night but one of the nights was a special one and unforgettable night.

In the night, Peter was so tired and dosed off. When he woke up in the morning, he found out that someone was sleeping beside him. He quickly and gently pulled himself from his position, after careful observing from a distance. He found out that the person was a mad man. He was scared but however, he just wanted to be sure that the person was okay. He picked up a long stick, and then he pocked the man gently but quickly. The man turned himself to the other side and said "Hello my friend." Peter quickly picked up his rucksack and ran away.

Chapter 12: Nowhere to Sleep

No one to talk to about my experience, when Peter reached his place of work, throughout his shift, the night memory didn't go away from him. It was difficult for him to fully concentrate at work, he was restless but however, he still tried to do his best. Soon, the night had fallen again and he had no alternative place to sleep than the uncompleted building. When Peter arrived at the building, he checked the surroundings to be sure that it is safe to sleep and no-one is around or inside it. It was hard for him to cope, especially when it rained. The funniest thing was that, he created a bed. The kind of the bed he used was secure to keep him safe from flooding. There were usually flooding in the rooms of the uncompleted building when it rains. The way in which the bed was fabricated appeared funny but Peter was dejected and was uncomfortable. He lay blocks on the floor in a corner of one of the rooms and laid flat woods on top of the block. It was hard for him to sleep at night, and he usually stayed awake at most nights. Since the madman incident, he became fearful and was frightened. Life in the uncompleted building was one of the hardest one, "I vowed to fight against such grim." Peter thought he would grow up someday, and wouldn't want to wish children to be in a situation such as his but, the tougher challenge still lies ahead, sometimes he wondered why he was still living. He felt, his childhood joy had been tampered with. One day, Lemmy met Peter in the bus stop. The bus stop was the place they first met. The place wasn't far away from the uncompleted building where Peter normally slept. In fact, it was about two minutes walking distance away from the building. Lemmy was happy to see him again but was surprised and wanted to know what he was doing at that same place, "Hi Peter, what are you doing here?"

"Good- morning sir" Peter's reply was gloomy and he didn't know what to say or do.

"Hum, hum," he was rambling in words and quickly said,

"I live here," he was speechless, dejected and did not know what to say but quickly replied, " no, I came to see someone." Noticing this, Lemmy knew that something was wrong, "Are you sure, and why did you dress this way? Are you not going to work today?" Asked Lemmy.

Peter looked terrible in the way in which he dressed and he was dirty too, his response to Lemmy's question caught him by surprise when he said, "I am on my way to work sir," said Peter. Without hesitation, Lemmy replied, "You mean, you are on your way to work, and you are dressed this way?" Peter wasn't wearing his uniform and Lemmy wasn't sure if he would be going to work or not, Peter replied, "Yes sir, my uniform is at work and the reason I left home early was to freshen myself at work." Lemmy wasn't comfortable with his reply and quickly said, "But you just told me that you came to see someone, so, do you stay here?" The question came to Peter as a shock and he wouldn't want anyone to know that he lived in the uncompleted building. He was afraid and troubled and rashly replied," No, Yes, No, sir, I meant I came to see someone."

He was confused and ashamed to tell him that he stayed in that uncompleted building next to the bus stop. Nevertheless, Lemmy looked straight into his eyes, shook his head. He felt Peter had lied to him. He then said, "Make sure you are not late."

"Okay sir," replied Peter.

Lemmy lived around the same area too and Peter was worried and wouldn't want to see him. Two days later, it was very early in the morning, precisely, 6:00am, someone called, "Peter" when the person approached him, he asked, "Peter, what are you doing here? So, this is where you slept, why have you lied to me?" Peter was despondent and sad, before he could say a word, Lemmy added, "You should have told me, you had no place to sleep." All Peter could say, was, "I am sorry sir."

"Sorry, nonsense, here is not safe for you and was that why you asked for nightshifts?" Asked Lemmy.

"Yes sir," replied Peter.

He then however, asked him to follow him. He took him to his house and told him to take his bath. Lemmy picked up the phone, and called Peter's department, where he worked to inform them that he would be coming late to work. After a while, he said to him, "Listen Peter, you will be going to the office with me." Not so long, they departed, when they got to his office, he took him to the operation department's office and explained Peter's situation. Lemmy pleaded on his behalf that he was changed from dayshift to the nightshift. Peter was immediately transferred from dayshifts to the nightshifts. He would be in the same company but, in the Company B.

The walking distance from Company A to B was three minutes. Lemmy told him, he is directly responsible in the management of Company B and would be visiting him there. After the processing had been made, Lemmy sent Peter away, "Go and finish your day shift at Company A, after your shift, make sure you meet me at my home".

Peter then left for his last dayshift. Arriving at work, peter informed his colleagues about the change. They were so happy for him and wished him well. After finishing the day shift, he left for Lemmy's place as predicted. Lemmy had a girlfriend called Tina, Peter was introduced to her. Peter wasn't expecting a surprise at this stage but was amused by Lemmy's gesture when he said, "Peter sleep here tonight, you are welcome at my place at anytime, my girlfriend and I have agreed to give you a spare key. You can come in and have a rest after your shift," He said, his girlfriend, Tina usually starts work at 9: 00am and finishes at 6:00pm Monday to Friday. The room was free for peter between 9:00am to 5:00pm. Peter was short of words and was elated. He thanked Lemmy and was grateful to him. There is something Peter wanted to find out and without hesitation, he asked, "How come that you know about the uncompleted building?" As a matter of fact, since last they met, Lemmy has been sniffing around to find out where peter had been sleeping. He said he told people to watch his movements.

A spare key was given to Peter and he passed the night at Lemmy's place. The next day Lemmy and Tina went to work and left him behind. When he woke up he cleaned the home and took his bath. Later, Peter took his breakfast. He was delighted and was extremely overjoyed, he said, "I have never been so thrilled." At 5:00pm he left for his night shift. While on his way to work, he was singing, he sang the song of joy, "I HAVE THE JOY, THE JOY OF MY LIFE, JOY EVERY DAY". People were watching and kept looking at him, he was singing loudly and was light-hearted. Peter couldn't realise that his voice was circulating everywhere. He resumed his shift precisely at 6:00pm, the nightshift was okay and he was taken round the new site and was told Lemmy was the site main supervisor at Company B. He was later introduced to meet new friends. Peter met Major and Thomas. People called one of them Major so he decided to call him Major too. Peter was told that Major and Thomas worked with another security firm. Major worked and lived in the same compound. Peter's main assignments were to patrol and protect the company, client's property from losses and theft. The nightshift was over and a new nightshift had just begun, after his shift, he went home. Lemmy was still at home, he was fast asleep, although Peter had been informed that he would be working nightshifts at Company B. Peter thought he could gently make some cooking. Unfortunately, Lemmy was such a man that wouldn't let Peter do housekeeping. As he advanced his feet, Lemmy asked. "What are you doing?" Peter thought he was still sleeping but was surprised that he was awake, he replied, "I want to clean the home and cook before I sleep." Lemmy didn't want him to do anything and told him, "Come-on Peter," he sent him to bed and said he must be tired. He added, "I will do the cooking and clean the home," said Lemmy.

Peter insisted and was about to clean the home, Lemmy jumped out of his bed and dragged him to the bed, just like a baby. Peter slept off. He later woke-up and felt very strong. Lemmy had already set the table for the meal, the housekeeping has been done. Immediately he noticed that Peter had woken-up, he said,

"Go and have your bath my friend, I am waiting for you. The table is set." It was marvellous, Peter was overjoyed and felt he had been treated as very important person (VIP), he quickly said, "Okay sir."

He couldn't be patient to take his bath, immediately, he jumped to the table. Peter was moved to tears and said, "I have never been treated with such dignity in my entire life," Lemmy laughed and said,

"Peter, you have went through a lot in your life, come-on let us eat we are now friends." Lemmy was such a nice man. The treatment he gave Peter was tremendous. This had remained in his memory till this day. Afterward, they both went out and later came back and prepared for their nightshift.

Chapter 13: Visit to the Village

The month has now ended and this was the time for me to fulfil my promise towards Mary. I always remembered I'd promised to give her my first salary and I thought I needed to see her in the village as soon as possible. I decided to visit Robert first, because I knew Mary sometimes visits him. Arriving at Robert's place, he said it was over three weeks she had visited the city. I then decided to travel to the village to see her. When I got to the village Tai, Janet and Mary were happy to see me. She rushed and hugged me, "Good-afternoon Mum," Peter said.

"I missed you Peter," she said. She had been in the city several times to visit Robert my friend and it was so difficult to see me because I'd always been busy at work.

" I missed you too mum," replied Peter. Since the last incident in the village, that was the first day we had an opportunity to stay together for a longer period. I stayed in the village for the weekend. A few hours after my arrival, I called Mary in private for a meeting, as I'd wanted to explain to her about my new job, before I could say a word, she said, "I was told about your new job and I was worried about your education." I knew she'd be worried, "Mum, I am worried too, but, what could I have done to help myself?" She knew I'd wanted to go to school too, and she'd prayed to live and see my success, "Not after all you've gone through," she said. Mary wouldn't stop telling me about how important it was for me to go back to school, our discussion was intensive that I became passionate about education affairs, as she was about to get nervous about the matter, I said, "Mum, don't worry I will be fine, no matter how long it'll take me, I will surely go back to school someday," said Peter. She always spoiled me with food and as I was thinking about it too, she said, "I think your food will soon be ready, I'd told Tai to prepare your favourite dish,"

"Thank you mum," replied Peter. I quickly told her the reason why I'd came to see her in the village. She was delighted when I told her I'd been paid and I'd brought my first wage to her as promised. She thanked me but however said, "you need the money more than I do, please keep it." She wouldn't collect the money, and we both started to struggle with it. After a few minutes, I said to her. "Mum, I know the way you feel about me, however, I vowed to give my first salary to you, please accept it," to me, it was an accomplishment sign of my promise, not after all she'd gone through for my sake. She wouldn't still accept the money but however gave me a condition, "I will accept it, but on one condition," said Mary. I was then curious to know in which condition she was referring to, I quickly asked, "What condition mum? I was completely surprised when she said, "For the past month I'd been saving some money as well, and I also promised to give them to you, anytime I set my eyes on you," said Mary. Hurriedly, she went into her room and brought the money in a white small envelope, "No mum, what kind of thing is this," Peter wasn't happy with her gesture either, "I told you I'd made a vow and yet, you wouldn't like to collect the money," said Peter. Mary claimed she'd made a vow too, however, we both decided to make a deal. "I will give you mine and you will give me yours," suggested Mary. I thought it was joke but she was very serious. I'd no choice left than to accept her deal.

"Okay mum, deal," said Peter. The sum she swapped for mine was twice the size of my wage. As soon as my day was over at the village and I was about to leave, I took part out of the money she gave to me and I put the rest in an envelope. I put the envelope under her pillow and put the following message on it for her to read.

Dear Mum,
This is a gift from your son please accept it with love. I love you, Peter.

Before I left the village, I was told a story. Mary told me, "It was all her fault," she said. After the death of Elizabeth, Tony my father decided not to remarry another woman. He however stayed single for six years. "It all started as a wisecrack", said Mary.

She told Tony, it was over six years now that he had been single without a wife. Mary remembered Tony always said he loved Elizabeth dearly and her children. Tony had decided to remain unmarried because he didn't want to share Elizabeth's love with any other woman. "It was a better thing for him to remain single." Mary said.

I also remembered saying to him, "We all know you love them so much, but, you cannot continue to be single forever besides, you need a wife to help you take care of your children," said Mary. Tony was a happy man the way he was and didn't require a new wife. He claimed.

Mary recollected having an argument about the same issues, she testified to the fact, how Tony used to love and care for Vincent, Joy and I. Sometimes, she would put Joy on his back, "He wouldn't let anyone touch her," said Mary. Things happened so quickly when Mary collided with family members. Everything that happened took Tony by surprise. The family carefully planned and delegated members to look for a wife for Tony in a neighbouring country Benin. Benin was one of the West African countries too. The capital city of Benin was then Coutonu but now is Port-Novo. The border line between Benin and Nigeria was Seme, the common name that people normally call the place was Seme border. Seme was about 30 minutes' drive faraway from Badagry Town, main roundabout. In fact, Mary was amongst the delegates that travelled across the border. I could remember that she took me along too. The Beninese official language was French. However, other dialects were spoken too. After reaching Coutonu, we then travelled to a remote village. We finally arrived at a village called Bonou. We toured other places such as Azowuse, Adjohoun, Dangbo and Danssa-Zoume. It was interesting, and it took us several days to go through those places. We did a lot of walking and took a canoe. There was no transport covering most of that area in those days. As a child, I wasn't really sure of what was actually going on, all I could remember was that, there were another two females that followed us back to Lagos city Nigeria. One of the women was so young and very beautiful. Mary knew exactly what Tony would prefer, Tony was at work when we arrived back home. As soon as he arrived and got sight of the young beautiful woman, he was melted in love. Immediately, Mary said, "I know your taste Tony, so we got you a wife." The temptation was powerful for Tony and he couldn't resist it, or either say no. Tony was just smiling and Beki was smiling too. "So, my son that was how it all started." She was so sorry that things went wrong, "Please forgive me." After narrating the story, she cried for several minutes and she regretted for all that had happened. She wished she could have turned the clock back. Nevertheless, I held her hands and showed appreciation for all she'd done on my behalf. I told her, "As I am concerned, nothing changes." Mary remained my mother, and it was difficult for me to perceive that she wasn't my biological mother. How could that be, to me, it was all a joke, "How could they suddenly tell me that Mary wasn't my real Mother?" My God, could you have believed them? I was told things which should have been told a long time ago. Do you know that she also said, Elizabeth had got children elsewhere before us? Maria and Jude were Elizabeth's children too. They were my half brother and sister. The funniest thing was that, the people I also thought were my distant family, happened to be my uncles and aunts. They were Elizabeth's brothers and sisters. Elizabeth had got two sisters and three brothers. She was the most senior amongst them. All I was told was like a day dream to me and no one could realise the trauma I was going through. Things started happening quickly, and the truth was now apparent, I didn't let that bother me anyway. After she had finished narrating the story, I finally departed from Akarakunmo Badagry. Mary promised to come to the city sometime. It was hard for me to understand.

Chapter 14: Cocoa Warehouse

As soon as Peter returned from the village, he went to his place of work. A few days later, he met Adam. He was the foreman, supervising the day's activities of Company B, cocoa warehouse. The place was a busy place. Trailers and Lorries often brought cocoa and cashew nuts from the farms. There were labourers on standby working in the warehouse. They would offload the goods in the trailers and store them in the cocoa and cashew warehouse. Later the cashew nuts and the cocoa would be loaded again in containers and would be transported to the Tin-can Island Port in Lagos. The goods would be later shipped abroad. A trailer normally carried about four hundred bags of cocoa and about three hundred bags of cashew nuts. The loading and offloading job was being carried out by the labourers. This was a hard labour work. The labourers would put the bags on their heads and walk or run about Ten to fifteen metres distance, before they could offload, and, or load the cocoa and cashew.

You must be very strong and energetic to do this kind of job. The labourers were always working in group of seven or ten. The only person that normally does the offloading and loading in those days were Ghanaians. They were strong and have got the spirit of endurance. They were always smiling while working. Peter was already looking forward to join the group. He then approached Adam the foreman. He told him of his interest to join the group. Adam was surprised and laughed at Peter, he thought Peter couldn't do such a job. He said to him, "You this small security boy, go away." Peter insisted and begged to do it. He would not give Adam a breathing space. Finally, Adam agreed to give it a try but he emphasised and advised that the stress would be too much. Peter remembered he spoke with his manager Steve before he could fully engage himself as one of Adam's labourers. Lemmy was informed too. Peter was now sixteen years old when he started working in the warehouse. He was so happy because he knew the job would give him an additional income. He normally started his night shifts at 6:00pm and closes at 6:00am in the morning, however, Lemmy had fixed his break at every 5:00am. This arrangement enabled Peter to have a rest before the start of the labourer job. The day job starts 9:00am and the warehouse closes at 4:00pm. Peter's first day at the cocoa warehouse was stressful as predicted. The cocoa bags were heavy and the cashew bags were heavier than the cocoa bags. My mates were surprised to see me in the group. There were four groups in the yard, which the labourers were about thirty-five in numbers. They were eight people in each group. The only Nigerian amongst the group was Adewale. He was caring too but later left the group to join the Nigerian Armed Forces. Sometimes, they normally offload and sometimes they do load cocoa in the containers. The cocoa in the container would be taken to the Tin-Can Island Port and would be shipped abroad. A few days later, Peter got used to the labourers job. They sang sometimes, and peter had made friends amongst his colleagues. Major arranged a small room for Peter and not so long peter started living at his place of work. They cooked outside, and it was fun, especially when Lemmy his friend was around. He started enjoying the place and he took his labourer job seriously. Peter started developing muscles and had grown up quickly due to the heavy loads.

One day, Peter visited Robert and he was told that Mary was in the city. He quickly went to Tony's place to see her. He was accompanied by Robert. When they got there, they were told that Mary had left for the village some few hours ago. Peter was delighted to see Joy and Joy was happy too. They quickly left in a haste because Peter wouldn't like to see Tony. Soon afterwards, Robert and Peter departed.

It had been a long time ago that Peter saw Vincent his brother, while, working in the cocoa warehouse, he saw someone positioned at a nearby distance. The person appeared to be Vincent and Peter could recollect that he had giving his work address to Joy during his last visit to Tony's Place. Peter was so happy when he took sight of him, Vincent could also observe that, and he quickly said, "Take it easy, and finish your job first." He had grown too and he should be at least twenty years old by now.

Peter was with the group, offloading a trailer of cocoa. After finishing offloading, he then made his way to him. They then went to a nearby restaurant. Vincent was upset to see Peter carrying heavy loads such as cocoa and cashew bags at his age. He then suddenly burst to tears and said, "Good to see you again," Joy told him all the maltreatment Peter had gone through. Vincent was dropped out of school too, his education was stopped and he was dumped in a mechanical workshop. He was an apprentice in a roadside mechanical garage. A few years later the family friend he was staying with died too, "I am alone and lonely too," said Vincent. Peter and Vincent discussed at length and later ate some food and they both departed in good faith. They were happy to see each other. It has been over six years they last met. Peter returned to the cocoa warehouse and continued his job. His time table was enjoyable and enabled him, sometimes to close at 3:00pm. The first thing he did was to put a mat on the floor and sleep off. He slept at least two to three hours everyday after his labourer job. When he woke up, he would then prepare for his security night duties. His shifts usually started at every 6:00pm. Lemmy his site supervisor was helpful too. He made his work enjoyable and flexible. Life at the cocoa warehouse was an unforgettable one.

Peter's close friends were Nana and Yanke, one day he had them discussing when was the next ship leaving to Europe. Peter had also heard the hearsay that boys from the cocoa warehouse normally hid in a ship and sailed to a European destination. For Yanke, that wasn't a problem. He knew the sailing plan, how, when and what to do. It was top secret amongst the Ghanaian cocoa workers. That very day, Peter caught Yanke and Nana discussing when the next ship was leaving but he couldn't figure out if what he was thinking was right. Peter heard Yanke saying, "I think in about two weeks' time." He wasn't sure what the topic was, but as soon as he moved nearer, he heard Nana saying too, "Start making preparations so that we don't miss the ship again." That was it and that had been the most interesting topic Peter had been looking forward to. A few minutes later Peter approached Yanke, that wasn't a problem to ask him questions, since they were friends, "Hi Yanke, I heard you saying something about a ship, can you please tell me more about it?" asked Peter. Suddenly fear came over him and he wouldn't like to speak about it. While he tried to deny it, Peter said, "I heard rumours, that, you have tried to board a ship to abroad," Yanke was under the assumption that Peter knew about it and couldn't lie to him since they were friends. He however replied, "Its stowaway." The name was new to Peter and it was the first time he heard about it, "What is that?" Peter asked. Without hesitation, his friend replied, "It means to conceal oneself in a ship or aircraft so as to travel without paying and it is done secretly." Replied Yanke. That was interesting for Peter and he wanted to know more about it, he quickly asked, "What do you mean, will you travel without paying, how come?"

"Yes" Replied Yanke. The ship will be departing from Tin-Can Island Port Lagos Nigeria in West Africa and would be heading to Europe. The ship would be stopping in Congo Sea Port and Gabon Sea Port. They would be offloading goods. Afterwards, the ship would be heading to Europe as its final destination. To Peter, this was too good to be true and, already, he had been looking forward to it, "Nana and I intended to stowaway with the next ship," said Yanke. When Peter heard that, he was pleased with what he heard, "Interesting," He said. Yanke was surprised at his action and could already start to read meaning to it, "Don't tell me you are interested?" Asked Yanke. My God, without hesitation, Peter replied loudly,

"YES OF COURSE, I AM INTERESTED." The task ahead was hard and Yanke thought Peter couldn't do it. There were a lot of risks with the trip and Yanke also thought Peter was too young to come with them. Peter was desperate and wouldn't want to miss the opportunity to go with Yanke. "What makes you feel; I can't do it?" Peter asked.

He wanted to know the risk and was curious to know everything about the journey. He persuaded him to tell him all he needed to know to get prepared for the trip.

They would be spending two to three weeks hiding in the ship. They would be there until their final destination. There would be no food or drink for the period. The only thing that was allowed was two tins of small sized evaporated milk and some peppermint sweets. "The milk and the sweets would keep us strong until we arrive at our destination," said Yanke.

It was not an easy task to board the ship. It was another risk entirely. You must be vigilant, if you are noticed that would be the end of your trip. There was always someone present at the main entrance of the ship "Gangway" before the ship departed from the Port, a fee must be paid to the gangway man. Gaining access through the gangway man was difficult and the only free ticket to your journey was to pay a little fee to the gangway man. After paying a fee, the gangway man would accompany you to a hiding place. Two to three are allowed to stowaway per a ship, you cannot be many in a ship. To stowaway, was a matter of life and death. Yanke thought he could scare Peter with these things, after feeding him with this information, he was surprised when Peter said, "It's okay by me, I will take the risk too." He thought Peter would be frightened with the risks associated with the trip. He tried to discourage Peter not to make the trip with them, "Peter I am sorry that you can't make it with us this time, the gangway man only wants two people," Nana and Yanke was to make the trip and Yanke advised Peter to try next time. "Besides, I don't want you to stowaway, you are too young to go with us," said Yanke. Peter was unhappy and would do anything to be part of Yanke's group, "Listen, I will be seventeen years old soon," Peter claimed, since Yanke could do it, he also felt he would be capable to handle it too, "What makes you think, I can't do it?" Peter asked. Yanke left him without a word.

Yanke and Nana were nice friends to Peter and they liked him very much. Two days later he came back to Peter, this was too good

to be a good news, "Peter, I have spoken with Nana and he said you can take his place," said Yanke. Peter was surprised that Nana gave away his place for him "Nana had decided to stowaway next time because he had experienced more than you," said Yanke. Peter was thrilled about the news. The journey was in three weeks' time and Peter was advised to prepare for it, "Please it's a secret." Peter was warned not to tell anyone about the plan.

To Peter, it was like a joke and dream impossible but a possible mission. He then started preparation. But, he thought some people needed to know about his journey. Peter remembered he had been warned to keep it secret but, what if something went wrong? By the way "who cares about me?" He then started thinking about the trip. Things kept coming to his memory, he thought no one cared about him, Peter recalled when he was having sleepless nights at the uncompleted building. What of, if anything bad had happened to him then? The abandoned vehicle, wandering the streets, was that not part of the mystery? While having thought of these things, something else came to his mind. What could that be? But, "Mary, Robert, Joy and Lemmy does care about me."

He knew if he told them about the trip, nobody would allow him to go. He was worried and confused and it took him a whole day to conclude on what to do. A few days later, Joy visited him at his work place. It was sad to hear that Tony was ill and "it was serious," said Joy. They had sent for Mary too, and thought Tony would soon die. However, Tony wasn't Peter's problem but Peter hoped to see soon at Tony's place.

Three days leading to Peter's trip. He went to Tony's place, when he got there, he met Beki crying. Peter thought Tony was dead. However, he was still alive. He greeted Beki, as soon as Mary and Joy heard his voice, they quickly, ran and hugged him. The reason

Peter went to Tony's place was to tell Mary and Joy that he would be travelling abroad. As soon as he broke the news, Mary was eager and wanted to know when was that going to be. She asked, "Which country are you going to?" Mary knew Peter didn't have money to enable him to travel abroad and was worried at the news.

Peter didn't know which country he would be heading to either. Peter had got his reason why he broke the news, he however said, "I don't want you to be scared that maybe, I had gone missing again." Peter consoled both of them not to be too worried about him "why wouldn't I be worried" Mary said, she claimed that Peter's dad's condition was bad, he was seriously ill and she thought it was not a good idea for him to leave him now." Mama, you must be joking." Did he care about him, yes, Peter was worried that he was ill but, he had made up his mind that nothing was going to prevent him not to make this trip. Mary was sad and quickly said "I am out of this," she wanted Peter to tell Tony about his plan and Peter wanted her to do that on his behalf, "Tell him yourself," said Mary. She didn't want to get involved with Tony's troubles, "Fine I will," replied Peter.

When Peter got into Tony's room, he was told he hadn't spoken for the past two days and they were preparing to take him to hospital in Abeokuta to conduct a test on him.

Abeokuta was one of the Yoruba States in Nigeria. Peter greeted Tony "good evening dad," he was imagining, even if he couldn't speak but at least he could hear him. Peter was sorry that he was ill and he wished him better. However, he was going abroad and he felt he should know about it anyway, "that is why, I am here." Peter wanted to make some kind of peace with Tony, since he would be away anyway. Peter asked Tony if they could be friends again, "I know you will not die, you will live to see me again," said Peter. Peter then bend his head and pecked him on his cheek. As soon as he was about to leave, it caught everyone by surprise when they heard him speak, "My son, please forgive me. I can't speak much, but I heard what you said," said Tony.

Peter then called Mary, Joy and Beki, but, Beki responded reluctantly. To him, he owned no grudges against anyone however, "would be in touch as soon as he arrived safely." Before Peter could finish talking, Beki had left anyway. He wasn't surprised either. Peter held Mary and Joy's hands and hugged them. They were crying and were unable to say a word. Without delay Peter left them for

good. It would be unkind for Peter not to see Robert before his departure, he later judged right to do so. He went to Robert's house and he explained the same thing to him. He was happy but sad at the same time because, he thought he would miss him.

On that same day evening, Peter went to work, his heart was troubled. He thought to explain to Lemmy might cause him trouble. He knew Lemmy was kind in heart and he appreciated all that he had done for him, "Lemmy is my site supervisor and my friend." It was uncomfortable for Peter not to tell him about his trip. After all he had done for him? Peter was still concerned about breaking the news, since it was a secret. Nevertheless, he however said it. This wasn't so surprising for Lemmy, he knew that most of the Ghanaians did it, "I know it's a stowaway," said Lemmy.

Lemmy knew Peter didn't have money to travel but advised him. He said, "Be careful, I wish all should go well with you." He was happy for me and couldn't stop him not to do it, "Peter, I am proud of you," said Lemmy. He was proud of Peter because he knew this was the first time in his entire life to see a native of Nigeria try to stowaway in a ship. Our shift continued until the next day.

Chapter 15: Run Away with a Ship

Time for a great battle, when I would be facing one of the biggest challenges of my life, it was a matter of life and death. On that day, Yanke my friend told me not to stress myself. The ship would be leaving on the next day evening, I was instructed by him on what to do and don't, "You must be at the sea port between 6:00am and 7:00am," said Yanke. At the Port, I was told to keep walking straight towards the ship," When you get there, you will see the gangway man waiting at the entrance. Remember to pay him and he will direct you on what to do," said Yanke. I was worried and quickly asked, "But, how can I identify the gangway man?" The journey had been carefully planned by Yanke, and my type of question wasn't a big deal to him. "Don't worry, he will give a signal," replied Yanke. Afterwards, Yanke continued to remind me of what to bring along and what not to bring. He told me to wear jeans and specified that, black jeans would be preferable however, he emphasised that I shouldn't be panicked. Lemmy was aware of the matter and told me not to do any work. He allowed me to have my rest for that night. I put my belongings together and wrote a letter with it. My letter was addressed to Mary and Joy. It was so difficult for me to fully make up my mind and I was downcast when I started writing,
(Lemmy Helped Me).

Dear Parents,

This is just the beginning of a new journey, new life, maybe my final moments on earth. I am sorry for the feeling this letter may cause however, I need to pour my feelings and my heart so that you will know what has happened to me.

I have suffered a lot, and my childhood rights have been denied. I slept in unpleasant places, in an abandoned vehicle, abandoned building and with strangers. A mad man kept me in company, while I was fast asleep. My childhood had seen shame and calamity, I begged for food in marketplaces and my life was full of mysteries of shocking news.

What could be so shocking when I heard that, the woman I use to know as my mother for the past fifteen years was not my real mother? My misfortune has pushed me to the wall. I had no alternative than to fight back.

I am sorry that I have to run away with a ship to an unknown destination, I don't know if I will make it. If I make it, I promise, you will be the first people to know. But, if I don't, don't worry. Just take it as my destiny.

Be warned not to do anything about this letter. Don't even try to take any further step, because if you do, you might be creating more problems for me. I love you all, please tell my father and Beki, I've forgiven them and no one should be blamed for my misfortune.

Hope to see you again. Mary, thank you for everything.

Bye
Your Son

After finishing writing the letter, the letter and my belongings were handed over to Lemmy. Time wasn't on my side and it was very late at night. I wasn't worried to catch up with sleep because I was told that there were lots of sleep that would catch up with us in the ship. At around 5:00am I finally departed with Lemmy. As soon as I arrived at the sea port around 6:30am, at the port entrance I saw Albert, I was scared and thought he was sent by Tony to prevent my journey. I wanted to run but, I decided to see him anyway. He saw me too and I quickly greeted him. He asked, "What are you doing here Peter?" I was dejected and thought it was all over. But I picked the courage to confront him. Immediately, I replied, "I work in a cocoa warehouse and we are called to offload goods here." I quickly asked him too, "and you what are you doing here?"

"I work here too," said Albert

"Okay Peter, see you soon." My God, thanks to Yanke that kept reminding me not to be panicked. I was relieved. Afterwards I made my way towards the entrance of the ship as instructed. You needed to see my face when I got to the main entrance of the ship. I was scared when I saw a man standing at the entrance. He was wearing a safety jacket. The man looked straight into my eyes and shook his head. He tapped his hand on his left and right legs and smiled. He directed me with the tip of his finger and pretended that he was talking to someone else. There were white men moving in and out of the ship too. Finally, I gained access into the ship. A few minutes later, the man came to me and collected some money. He hid me, not too far from the cocoa bags that were already in the ship. They were to be shipped to European countries. He then later showed me my future hiding place, this was between the cocoa that was at the left side corner of the ship.

I was instructed and was restricted not to move from my location. I was surprised when he said "your friend Yanke is already hiding somewhere as well." I was later told that the ship would be leaving on that same day evening. Unfortunately, the ship didn't leave until the next day. I was then worried, what if anything goes wrong? I then started thinking and doubting if truly Yanke had made it to the ship or not.

But, what of if he was not in the ship?

Peter was completely worried and had got no experience relating to stowaways but he managed the situation with calm. But how long could he remain calm, he was now running out of patience and started thinking of how to get out of his hiding place. But, what of if Yanke was in the ship? Was it not that Peter would be destroying their plan? As he was under the impression to make his final decision on what to do, he heard a noise. The main ship entrance gate was now being closed down. Peter had no choice than to live to his fate.

After a few minutes Peter started hearing people's movements. He remembered the voices he heard were much closer to where he was hidden. The voices heard could have been the sailors.

When it was around 00.00hrs, Peter heard someone calling his name quietly.

"Peter." It was Yanke. He told Peter to come out of his hiding place and showed him the same place that was already shown to him by the gangway man. While they were still talking, they saw someone and later they saw another person. At first, they were scared but, later found out that the people, whom they saw, were stowaways too. Afterwards we went and hid behind the cargo while in hiding, they found additional two people. They were now six stowaways' boys hiding in the ship. They introduced themselves. The people they met were Kofi, Texan, Kwasi and Matthew.

All of them including Yanke were Ghanaians and Peter was the only one singled out as a Nigerian. "It was unusual to see a Nigerian to stowaway on a ship" the group said, they were all happy to see Peter on-board.

Kofi and Yanke were more experienced and Kofi was chosen as our team leader based on his experience. Kofi told the group that, the ship would be stopping at Congo in the next two to three days period. All cargos would be offloaded in Congo. The only thing that would be left was the cocoa that were meant to go to European countries. The cocoa would be their final hiding place. After Congo, the ship would be heading to Port- Gentil in Gabon. However, they couldn't identify the cargos that would be offloaded in Gabon. They were all worried that the cocoa hiding place was not spacious enough to contain the six of them. Meanwhile, it was so difficult to gain access to any other place and where the cocoa was. The cargo heading to Congo was blocking the whole place and there was no space for passage either. The only available hiding place was on the top of the cargo heading to Congo. They all held hands and agreed on what to do. After then Kofi gave the group an instruction on what to do and what to expect. They were told that, soon they would be getting to Congo and the goods would be offloaded at Congo sea port.

The only hiding place would be the cocoa heading to Europe. At this stage "Yanke and I will go and look for an alternative hiding place," said Kofi. Kofi thought they must hide somewhere quickly, if not they would be caught.

Kofi and Yanke made their way to look for a new hideout. Life wasn't easy in the ship. Spending a few days was like spending an entire life in hardship. No water to drink, no food to eat, the only thing they had was the peppermint sweet and the milk. Everything they had got was combined together. To urinate became a problem. Peter remembered that, he cried before he could urinate. He was in severe pain below his abdomen. Their situation was a terrible one. That was Texan and Peter's first experience as a stowaway.

Peter was vomiting on the first two days of the journey. His situation was so bad that he moaned and complained. He wanted to go back home if he could have saw a way out. Everyone was going

through the same hardship. Peter was however, encouraged by the experienced stowaway boys. Texan was ill too. As a matter of fact, Peter wanted to make Pooh and was immediately warned to hold it. There was no place to do pooh. It was not allowed for a stowaway to do pooh while on-board. That was why they were not allowed to eat anything. The pooh would smell and the odour would circulate everywhere. They would be caught out immediately.

What could he have done? He was uncomfortable and started crying. His condition became worse that he became constipated. His urine became yellow, and later became brown. Afterwards, Peter couldn't urine, his bowel was empty. They were all thirsty for water. One of them tried to get into the sailor's kitchen while they were all asleep at night. He wanted to get them water to drink. The kitchen door was locked.

When Kofi and Yanke came back, the only hiding place that was available was the hole. The hole was located at the side of the ship. The hole was where the fan that supplies the ship's air was situated.

This was in the middle, side of the ship. In the hole there was a staircase. The staircase leads to another small hole. In that small hole, was a big fan and the fan supplies air from the sea while the ship is on the move, and the air would come through the hole, and the air would circulate through the other hole and travel inside the ship. The air was used to keep goods safe while the ship travels.

Kofi explained in detail. Afterwards, Yanke advised the group "to get to the hole we have to walk straight along the ship's side, on top of the cargo and move starting from where we are currently located. Afterwards, we must turn around to the other side."

It was easy to gain access through the hole because they were on top of the cargo heading to Congo. The cargo in which they were on top was four to five meters high and the hole from the ground floor of the ship was about eight to eleven meters or more high.

"It would be difficult to come down after the Congo cargos would have been offloaded," said Kofi. They were unhappy and frightened and had got no other choice than to jump down from the ship side hole. However, they all agreed to take the risk. Their time was now running out and they needed to hurry up before the ship got to Congo's seaport. Without hesitation, they then made their way towards the hole. Peter's position was number three from the hole, leading towards outside, "the sea" and numbers four from the ship's hole entrance, "circulating air inside the ship." Yanke was number one, followed by Matthew, Peter, Texan, Kwasi and Kofi.

When they got to the hole, they had been instructed to line up according to their numbers. They would be lined up on the staircase and would stand there as long as the ship would remain in the Congolese sea port. The breeze from the hole was too powerful that it was pushing them against the iron bars of the ship. They had to hold the staircase handle very tightly so that they wouldn't be swung around.

A few hours later, the ship arrived at Congo, and before the ship headed for shore, the rate of the powerful fan reduced. It was a horrible experience for them, their bodies were shaken. Their lips and cheeks were swollen. They kept silent in the hole and Kofi their team leader kept close observation monitoring the activities. They were not allowed to talk to each other but could only whisper to one person and that person would carry it on and again and again.

Not too long, they got a signal from their leader "guys, all the goods have been offloaded and the only thing remaining there was the cocoa situated just before the middle of the ship and a car," said Kofi.

Later that evening the ship sailed and the powerful fan started again. Their clothes were so dirty, a few hours later they were instructed on what to do. To get out of the hole everyone must lean and hold tight against the wall and slide down gently. Meanwhile, it was organised that Kofi would jump down and watch if the coast was clear. He would later give a signal for the next person to jump down and he would go. The person that Kofi helped would do the same and go to the cocoa hideout. This would continue until no one was left behind. When it was Peter's turn, "I did as planned, but I fell down and collapsed for a few minutes" The group were scared and thought that would be the end of the trip. Kofi quickly ran and dragged him towards the back of the cocoa. He shook him heavily and called his name gently "Peter" until he regained consciousness. Yanke was still in the hole and waiting for a signal however, Kofi assisted him to climb the cocoa. He took him to join the others at the cocoa hideout. Kofi then went back to assist the other people left in the hole. The cocoa hiding place was modified and reconstructed by Yanke and Kofi. The cocoa was used to form a deep hole from top to far down. It was constructed in such a way that would be difficult to be noticed that people were inside. Unfortunately, the place wasn't big enough to contain more than five people. It was difficult to stand, and they could only sit-down. The cocoa hideout could only contain, Texan, Kofi, Yanke, Kwasi and Peter. There was no place for Matthew to hide, nevertheless, there was still a car left in the ship and he volunteered to hide separately inside the car. Time was running fast and the ship would soon arrive in Port-Gentil, They were all tired and there was still over two weeks to spend before they got to Europe. To date, we had spent six days and had got about a day or more to Gabon's Port.

Finally, the ship approached the harbour, and when the ship got to the port, we were all surprised at what happened. A forklift machine came inside the ship and went straight were the car was parked. Matthew was still hiding inside the car and before he could notice it, he was captured by the Gabonese people, the sailors came over. They were surprised at what they saw.

A couple of seconds later, the Gabonese came looking if there were still people hiding in the ship. They searched every place and every corner of the ship. It was easy to know where to focus on, the only hiding place that remained was the cocoa' place. Before they could advance towards our hideout, Kofi said, "Guys, just find your way out from this place, remember, and don't betray each other."

While he was still briefing us, everyone has started jumping down from the hideout. All of us went through a different way. I jumped down and fell on the floor for the second time. I was tired and weak, and I thought, "Courage, yes, I need courage." Immediately, I stood up on my two feet and I saw people running up and down. They were shouting and were speaking in a French language. They were every where. I tried to blend with them but couldn't figure out what they were up to. But I could imagine that they were saying perhaps, STOP HIM. I tried to repeat what they were saying. As I was doing so, they were running towards me. I ran and ran too. They were pointing their fingers toward me. I tried to point my fingers too. While doing so, my two legs kept moving left and right and I was staggering. My movement wasn't steady. Finally I fell on the floor, just at the main entrance of the ship. They were with big sticks and iron bars and before they could start beating me with it, the sailors

and the commander of the ship swung in. They lifted me up and took me to an existing prison already inside the ship.

When I got there I saw Kofi, Yanke, Matthew and Texan. I was told that Kwasi made it through the entrance. Kwasi was the only person that escaped amongst the six of us. We were interviewed by the commander and the captain of the ship.

We were asked series of questions, where did you board the ship from?

"From West Africa."

Were you all together?"

"No sir, we all met each other in the ship."

Where were you heading to?

"Europe." Hearing Europe, the commander said, "To Europe, I am sorry that you can no longer continue the journey with us." They handed us over to the Gabonese police. We were detained by them as was indicated by the ship commander. The commander said, "Our Company will arrange the necessary paperwork for your deportation." To him, he was sorry that we would be deported back to West Africa.

On hearing what they had said, we were then convinced that it was all over. We then requested for water, and it was over a week now, that we had drunk water.

This was it and it was all over now. We couldn't believe what had just happened to us not after all we had gone through, "when will all this pain end?" asked Peter.

In fact, we would soon be arrested and would be deported. What would that have meant for Peter? My God, the Gabonese police officers had arrived, they were called GENDARME and we were handcuffed. Yanke was handcuffed together with Matthew, Kofi was handcuffed together with Texan and I was handcuffed alone. Afterwards, we were taken to the Gendarmerie van. They took us to the police station and their station was called GENDARMARIE.

This was the first time Peter was handcuffed in his entire life. He then cried in horror. What a life? Where this misfortune would lead him? "Somebody help me," Peter cried.

Peter was handcuffed

After my arrest, terrible things happened to me at the hands of the Gabonese Gendarme. This is just the beginning of a new chapter. There are things that people go through that are beyond human imagination. Be patient to find out what that could have been for me. Part two of my book is full of many things. The autobiography is an educative story and inspiration. Don't miss out on reading my second book!

Message from the Author

I was unstable at school between the ages of 5 to 13 and I left school aged 14. When I was in school, I did not pay particular attention in class. My English was not very good, and I struggled to convey myself the way I wanted to. When I arrived in the UK, I had to attend Maths & English classes in order to improve my English. Nevertheless, I have received positive comments from the readers and fans of my book. I have also received comments from lecturers at higher institutions, where I was very encouraged. These kind words have prompted me to do some editing to the Unexpected Truth.

The editing of this book does not affect the book's originality or the narrative of the story. All I've done is sort out the punctuation and made anything ambiguous less so. This book was first published and printed in softcover by Author House UK Ltd on 21/11/2009, but the edited version of this book, in which you hold in your hands, was published by LASALA (Live and Survived and Live Again-(myself)). This book was created using the Lulu creative publishing service.

In reflection of my life and the struggle that comes with it, it is difficult to rule the pen out of existence. Would I say I'm done with it? And, who will ever tell what there's to tell? And, what goodness the months will bring?

To my fans and lovers of my books, this is just the beginning of a new journey in my life. Why must you be a part of this? Read my first and second book, I promise, you will not be disappointed. Hold on in expectation of the next, and the next, until there is no next. To everyone, there is always something new to take away from my poetry works and my books. What's next? My memoirs! See you soon!"

Over the years, I have published various academic papers. You can access some of these publications using these links or contact me at lasalafoundation@gmail.com or on Facebook at https://www.facebook.com/oluwafemisenubooks.

My Academic Publications

A CRITICAL ASSESSMENT OF ANTI-CORRUPTION STRATEGIES FOR ECONOMIC DEVELOPMENT IN SUB-SAHARAN AFRICA (DPR 2019) by Oluwafemi Senu

https://onlinelibrary.wiley.com/doi/abs/10.1111/dpr.12442

A short summary in the author's words: In this article, I assess the setbacks found in anti-corruption strategies to clarify the nuances of these for economic development in sub-Saharan Africa (SSA). I do this by asking questions such as how and in what conditions these anti-corruption strategies function in SSA. I use the United Nations Convention Against Corruption for my analyses. I explore the cases of Kenya and Nigeria to illuminate the gaps found in anti-corruption strategies on one hand, and on the other hand, I examine the challenges faced by the Department for International Development. I conclude by revealing the shortcomings found in development policies in the face of corrupt environments.

AFRICAN SCHOOL OF THOUGHT: THE MISSING IDEOLOGY IN FINDING A SOLUTION TO SUB-SAHARAN AFRICAN INSECURITY (DPR 2018)

Oluwafemi Senu & Folarin Daranijoh

https://onlinelibrary.wiley.com/doi/full/10.1111/dpr.12397

ASOT questions years of development policies aimed at Africa's economic challenges and human insecurities. In particular, questions are raised about the ideological functions, ideas and epistemological foundations in which policies are grounded. ASOT provides evidence that Africa's development pathways have ultimately been based on very limited ideas or have excluded ideals that underpin the political systems of countries in SSA.

ASOT draws attention to a pressing need for the inclusion of a new ideology capable of deconstructing unworkable policies in SSA. The paper also raises questions such as: what are the dangers of ideological functions? And how do we resolve or mitigate Africa's economic challenges and human insecurities?

Anticorruption Publications Online

November 2016 – AFROLEAKS: Tackling Corruption in Africa – Concluding the Case on Poverty: https://nactpvs.wordpress.com/2016/11/13/afroleaks-tackling-corruption-in-africa-concluding-the-case-on-poverty/

November 2016 – AFROLEAKS: Tackling Corruption in Africa – Sierra Leone Faces the SDGs [Part II]: https://nactpvs.wordpress.com/2016/11/06/afroleaks-tackling-corruption-in-africa-sierra-leone-faces-the-sdgs-part-ii/

October 2016 – AFROLEAKS: Tackling Corruption in Africa – Sierra Leone Faces the SDGs: https://nactpvs.wordpress.com/2016/10/30/afroleaks-tackling-corruption-in-africa-sierra-leone-faces-the-sdgs/

October 2016 – AFROLEAKS: Tackling Corruption in Africa – The SDGs Target Peace [Part II]: https://nactpvs.wordpress.com/2016/10/23/afroleaks-tackling-corruption-in-africa-the-sdgs-target-peace-part-ii/

October 2016 – AFROLEAKS: Tackling Corruption in Africa – The SDGs Target Peace [Part I]: https://nactpvs.wordpress.com/2016/10/16/afroleaks-tackling-corruption-in-africa-the-sdgs-target-peace-part-i/

October 2016 – AFROLEAKS: Tackling Corruption in Africa – The SDGs Target Equality [Part II]: https://nactpvs.wordpress.com/2016/10/09/758/

October 2016 – AFROLEAKS: Tackling Corruption in Africa – The SDGs Target Equality: https://nactpvs.wordpress.com/2016/10/02/afroleaks-tackling-corruption-in-africa-the-sdgs-target-equality/

September 2016 – AFROLEAKS: Tackling Corruption in Africa – The Sustainable Development Goals: https://nactpvs.wordpress.com/2016/09/25/afroleaks-tackling-corruption-in-africa-the-sustainable-development-goals/

September 2016 – AFROLEAKS: Tackling Corruption in Africa – The End of the Millennium Development Goals: https://nactpvs.wordpress.com/2016/09/18/afroleaks-tackling-corruption-in-africa-the-end-of-the-millennium-development-goals/

September 2016 – AFROLEAKS: Tackling Corruption in Africa – Economic Partnership Agreements [Part III]: https://nactpvs.wordpress.com/2016/09/11/afroleaks-tackling-corruption-in-africa-economic-partnership-agreements-part-iii/

September 2016 – AFROLEAKS: Tackling Corruption in Africa – Economic Partnership Agreements [Part II]: https://nactpvs.wordpress.com/2016/09/04/afroleaks-tackling-corruption-in-africa-economic-partnership-agreements-part-ii/

August 2016 – AFROLEAKS: Tackling Corruption in Africa – Economic Partnership Agreements [Part I]: https://nactpvs.wordpress.com/2016/08/28/afroleaks-tackling-corruption-in-africa-economic-partnership-agreements-part-i/

August 2016 – AFROLEAKS: Tackling Corruption in Africa – What about the Judiciary?: https://nactpvs.wordpress.com/2016/08/21/afroleaks-tackling-corruption-in-africa-what-about-the-judiciary/

August 2016 – AFROLEAKS: Tackling Corruption in Africa – Why Steal something that Belongs to you?: https://nactpvs.wordpress.com/2016/08/14/afroleaks-tackling-corruption-in-africa-why-steal-something-that-belongs-to-you/

August 2016 – AFROLEAKS: Tackling Corruption in Africa – An Overview of the Inner Problems: https://nactpvs.wordpress.com/2016/08/07/%ef%bb%bf%ef%bb%bfafroleaks-tackling-corruption-in-africa-an-overview-of-the-inner-problems/

July 2016 – AFROLEAKS: Tackling Corruption in Africa – An Introduction: https://nactpvs.wordpress.com/2016/07/31/afroleaks-tackling-corruption-in-africa-an-introduction/

July 2016 – AFROLEAKS: Foreign Aid and Corruption [Part II]: https://nactpvs.wordpress.com/2016/07/24/afroleaks-foreign-aid-and-corruption-part-ii/

July 2016 – AFROLEAKS: Foreign Aid and Corruption [Part I]: https://nactpvs.wordpress.com/2016/07/17/afroleaks-foreign-aid-and-corruption-part-i/

July 2016 – AFROLEAKS: Understanding Africa's Scale of Corruption – A Review of the Anti-Corruption Summit London 2016 [Part VI]: https://nactpvs.wordpress.com/2016/07/10/afroleaks-understanding-africas-scale-of-corruption-a-review-of-the-anti-corruption-summit-london-2016-part-vi/

July 2016 – AFROLEAKS: Understanding Africa's Scale of Corruption – A Review of the Anti-Corruption Summit London 2016 [Part V]: https://nactpvs.wordpress.com/2016/07/03/afroleaks-understanding-africas-scale-of-corruption-a-review-of-the-anti-corruption-summit-london-2016-part-v/

June 2016 – AFROLEAKS: Understanding Africa's Scale of Corruption – A Review of the Anti-Corruption Summit London 2016 [Part IV]: https://nactpvs.wordpress.com/2016/06/26/afroleaks-understanding-africas-scale-of-corruption-a-review-of-the-anti-corruption-summit-london-2016-part-iv/

June 2016 – AFROLEAKS: Understanding Africa's Scale of Corruption – A Review of the Anti-Corruption Summit London 2016 [Part III]: https://nactpvs.wordpress.com/2016/06/19/afroleaks-understanding-africas-scale-of-corruption-a-review-of-the-anti-corruption-summit-london-2016-part-iii/

June 2016: AFROLEAKS: Understanding Africa's Scale of Corruption – A Review of the Anti-Corruption Summit London 2016 [Part II]: https://nactpvs.wordpress.com/2016/06/12/afroleaks-understanding-africas-scale-of-corruption-a-review-of-the-anti-corruption-summit-london-2016-part-ii/

June 2016 – AFROLEAKS: Understanding Africa's Scale of Corruption – A Review of the Anti-Corruption Summit London 2016 [Part I]: https://nactpvs.wordpress.com/2016/06/05/afroleaks-understanding-africas-scale-of-corruption-a-review-of-the-anti-corruption-summit-london-2016-part-i/

May 2016 – AFROLEAKS: Do Anti-Corruption Initiatives Pose a Success or Challenge to Nigeria's Modern Democracy? [Part II]: https://nactpvs.wordpress.com/2016/05/29/afroleaks-do-anti-corruption-initiatives-pose-a-success-or-challenge-to-nigerias-modern-democracy-part-ii/

May 2016 – AFROLEAKS: Do Anti-Corruption Initiatives Pose a Success or Challenge to Nigeria's Modern Democracy? [Part I]: https://nactpvs.wordpress.com/2016/05/23/afroleaks-do-anti-corruption-initiatives-pose-a-success-or-challenge-to-nigerias-modern-democracy-part-I/

May 2016 – AFROLEAKS: What exactly are we talking about when we say 'fight against corruption?' [Part II]: https://nactpvs.wordpress.com/2016/05/16/afroleaks-what-exactly-are-we-talking-about-when-we-say-fight-against-corruption-part-ii/

May 2016 – AFROLEAKS: What exactly are we talking about when we say 'fight against corruption?' [Part I]: https://nactpvs.word-press.com/2016/05/09/afroleaks-what-exactly-are-we-talking-about-when-we-say-fight-against-corruption/

Photos

Peter Positioned left-
Tony in the Middle-
Vincent in the back
-Joy on the Right

Elizabeth & Tony in 1950s

 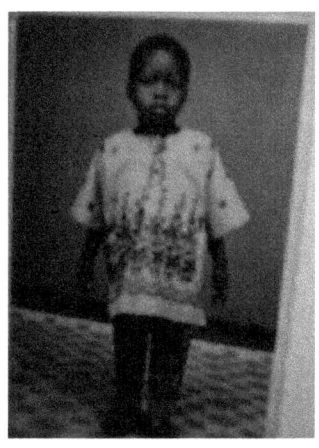

Mary Pedetin Senu. Peter Aunt think?

Peter, I guess at 4 but what do you

www.ingramcontent.com/pod-product-compliance
Lightning Source LLC
Chambersburg PA
CBHW071217160426
43196CB00012B/2333